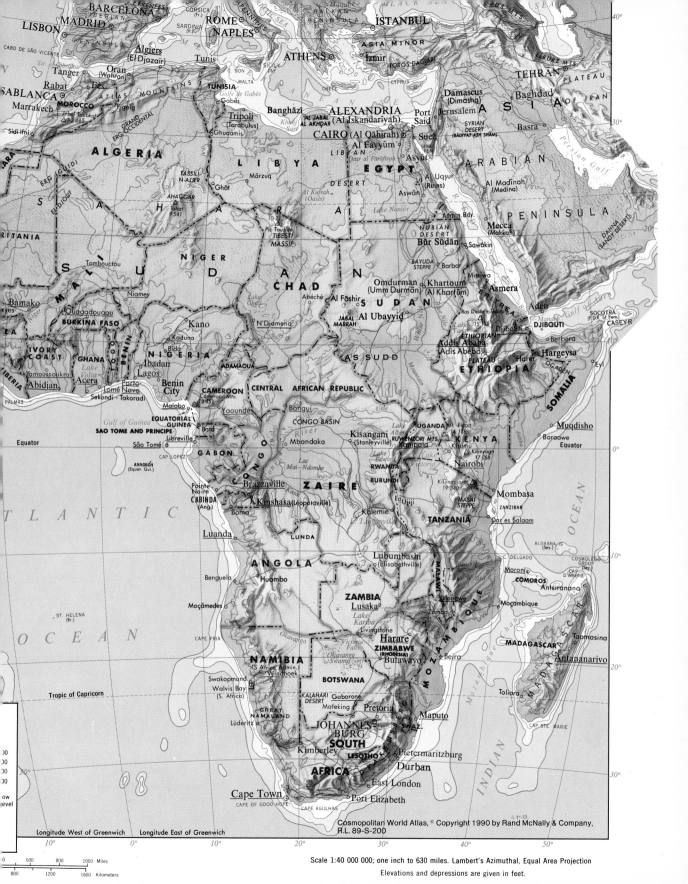

LISBON  MADRID  BARCELONA  CORSICA  ROME  BALKAN PENINSULA  ISTANBUL  BLACK SEA

CABO DE SÃO VICENTE  SARDINIA (It.)  NAPLES  ASIA MINOR

Algiers (El Djazair)  Tunis  ATHENS  Izmir  TEHRAN  PLATEAU  ELBURZ MTS.

Tanger  Oran (Wahran)  SICILY  CYPRUS  TOROS DAGLARI  OF IRAN

CASABLANCA  Rabat  Fès  MALTA  Damascus (Dimashq)  Baghdad

Marrakech  MOROCCO  C. BON  Banghāzi  ALEXANDRIA (Al Iskandariyah)  Jerusalem  ASIA  Basra

Sidi Ifni  Tripoli (Tarabulus)  AL JABAL AL AKHDAR  Port Said  SYRIAN DESERT (BADIYAT ASH SHAM)  Persian Gulf

ALGERIA  LIBYA  CAIRO (Al Qāhirah)  Suez  ARABIAN  DAHNA (SANDY DESERT)

Al Fayyūm  LIBYAN  Asyūt  PENINSULA

TASSILI N-AJJER  Ghāt  Mārzuq  DESERT  Al Uqsur (Ruins)  Mecca (Makkah)

AHAGGAR  Aswān  Al Madīnah (Medina)

Pic Toussidé  TIBESTI MASSIF  Lake Nasser  Bûr Sūdan  NUBIAN DESERT  SOCOTRA (P.D.R. of Yem.)

Tambouctou  NIGER  CHAD  BAYUDA STEPPE  Barbar  Sawākin  CASEYR

Niamey  Lake Chad  Abéché  Al Fāshir  Omdurman (Umm Durmān)  Khartoum (Al Khartūm)  Mitsiwa  Asmera  Aden  GULF OF ADEN

BURKINA FASO  Kano  N'Djamena  SUDAN  JABAL MARRAH  Al Ubayyid  Ras Dashen Terara 15 158  DJIBOUTI

Ouagadougou  Kaduna  ETHIOPIAN  Djibouti  Berbera

IVORY COAST  GHANA  NIGERIA  Bida  ADAMAOUA  AS SUDD  Addis Ababa (Adis Abeba)  PLATEAU  Harēr  Hargeysa  Eyl

Yamoussoukro  Ibadan  Benin City  CENTRAL AFRICAN REPUBLIC  ETHIOPIA  OGADEN

Abidjan  Lagos  Cameroon Mtn. (3 45)  Bangui  Uele  SOMALIA

Accra  Lomé  Porto-Novo  CAMEROON  CONGO BASIN  UGANDA  Mt. Elgon 14 178  Muqdisho

C. PALMAS  Sekondi-Takoradi  Malabo  Yaoundé  Kisangani (Stanleyville)  RUWENZORI MTS.  Kampala  KENYA  Baraawe  Equator

EQUATORIAL GUINEA  Bata  Mbandaka  Lake Albert  Kisumu  Kirinyaga 17 058  Nairobi

SAO TOME AND PRINCIPE  Libreville  Lake Edward  RWANDA  Lake Victoria  Kilimanjaro 19 340

Equator  São Tomé  CAP LOPEZ  GABON  CONGO  Lac Mai-Ndombe  BURUNDI  MASAI STEPPE  Mombasa

ANNOBÓN (Equat. Gui.)  Brazzaville  ZAIRE  Lualaba  Kalemie  ZANZIBAR

Pointe Noire  Kinshasa (Léopoldville)  Lake Tanganyika  TANZANIA  Dar es Salaam  ALDABRA IS. (Sey.)

CABINDA (Ang.)  Boma  COSMOLEDO GROUP (Sey.)  CAP D'AMBRE

Luanda  LUNDA  Lubumbashi (Elisabethville)  C. DELGADO  Moroni  Antsiranana

ANGOLA  COMOROS

Benguela  Huambo  ZAMBIA  MALAWI  Moçambique  MADAGASCAR  Toamasina

Moçâmedes  Lusaka  Lilongwe  MOZAMBIQUE

ST. HELENA (Br.)  Lake Kariba  Zomba

ATLANTIC OCEAN  Livingstone  Beira  Antananarivo

CAPE FRIA  Victoria Falls  Okavango Swamp  Harare  ZIMBABWE (RHODESIA)  Bulawayo

NAMIBIA (S. Africa Admin.)  Okavango  Taolaña  MADAGASCAR  CAP STE. MARIE

Swakopmund  Windhoek  BOTSWANA  Tropic of Capricorn

Walvis Bay (S. Africa)  KALAHARI DESERT  Gaborone  Maputo

GREAT NAMALAND  Mafeking  Pretoria  SWAZ.

Lüderitz  JOHANNESBURG  SOUTH  Maputo

Kimberley  LESOTHO  Pietermaritzburg

AFRICA  Durban

Cape Town  East London

CAPE OF GOOD HOPE  Port Elizabeth

CAPE AGULHAS

Cosmopolitan World Atlas, © Copyright 1990 by Rand McNally & Company, R.L. 89-S-200

Longitude West of Greenwich  Longitude East of Greenwich

10°  0°  10°  20°  30°  40°  50°

600  800  1000 Miles

800  1200  1600 Kilometers

Scale 1:40 000 000; one inch to 630 miles. Lambert's Azimuthal, Equal Area Projection

Elevations and depressions are given in feet.

*Enchantment of the World*

# MALAWI

*By Martha S.B. Lane*

---

**Consultant for Malawi:** John Rowe, Ph.D., African Studies Faculty, Northwestern University, Evanston, Illinois

**Consultant for Reading:** Robert L. Hillerich, Ph.D., Bowling Green State University, Bowling Green, Ohio

 CHILDRENS PRESS ®

CHICAGO

*Farmers burn a cane field to clear it for new planting.*

**Picture Acknowledgments**
**AP/Wide World Photos:** 55, 56, 58, 59, (2 photos), 75, 95
**Bruce Coleman Incorporated:** © **Dale & Marian Zimmerman,** 28
© **Virginia Grimes:** 12, 25 (top & bottom left)
**Historical Pictures Service, Chicago:** 41 (left), 43, 49 (left), 92
© **Martha S. B. Lane:** 5, 90, 91
**North Wind Picture Archives:** 32, 36, 37, 38, 41 (right), 42, 53
© **Photri:** Cover, Cover Inset, 8, 16, 19 (2 photos), 22, 29, 30, 44, 46, 49 (right), 60, 63, 64, 66 (2 photos), 67 (2 photos), 68, 69, 70, 72, 79, 80 (2 photos), 81, 98 (right), 99, 101 (left), 105, 111, 121
**Root Resources:** © **Loren M. Root,** 21 (left); © **Ted Farrington,** 23 (top); © **Stan Osolinski,** 27 (top left); © **Kenneth W. Fink,** 27 (bottom left)
**Shostal Associates/SuperStock International, Inc.:** 4, 6, 10, 15, 17, 65, 76, 85, 97 (right), 100, 107, 108, 114, 122
**Tom Stack & Associates:** © **Joe McDonald,** 23 (bottom left), 24 (bottom left), 25 (top right); © **Charles G. Summers, Jr.,** 24 (bottom right)
**Valan:** © **Stephen J. Krasemann,** 21 (right), 24 (top left); © **Alan Wilkinson,** 23 (bottom right); © **Pierre Mineau,** 24 (top right); © **Aubrey Lang,** 25 (bottom right), 26 (left); © **R. D. Stevens,** 26 (right); © **Arthur Christiansen,** 27 (right); © **Joyce Photographics,** 97 (top left); © **Val & Alan Wilkinson,** 97 (bottom left); © **Anthony Scullion,** 98 (left), 101 (right)
**Len W. Meents:** Maps on pages 15, 69
**Courtesy Flag Research Center, Winchester, Massachusetts 01890:** Flag on back cover
**Cover:** Zomba Plateau
**Cover Inset:** Market at Zomba

**Library of Congress Cataloging-in-Publication Data**

Lane, Martha S. B.
   Malawi / by Martha S.B. Lane.
      p.      cm. — (Enchantment of the world)
   Includes index.
   Summary: Introduces the geography, history,
government, lifestyles, and industries of Malawi.
   ISBN 0-516-02720-4
   1. Malawi—Juvenile literature.  [1.  Malawi.]
I. Title. II. Series.
DT3174.L35   1990                          89-25433
968.97—dc20                                    CIP
                                                   AC

*A market in Zomba*

## TABLE OF CONTENTS

*Senga Bay on Lake Malawi*

## Chapter 1

# MALAWI, LAND OF
# LAKE AND FIRE

---

Malawi is a landlocked country lying in the heart of Africa at the meeting point of the regional boundaries of East, Central, and Southern Africa. To the north lies Tanzania; to the northwest lies Zambia; and to the west, south, and southeast Malawi sits in a cradle formed by the boundaries of Mozambique. Malawi is one of the smallest countries in Africa, covering only 45,747 square miles (118,484 square kilometers). It is about the size of the state of Tennessee and about three-quarters the size of Great Britain. Like Tennessee, Malawi is long and narrow. It stretches about 520 miles (837 kilometers) from north to south and is only about 100 miles (161 kilometers) wide at its widest point in the central region. Just over one-quarter of the country, 9,300 square miles (24,087 square kilometers), is covered by water. Most of the water is contained in Lake Malawi, the country's most prominent natural feature.

Lake Malawi, or Lake Nyasa, is the third-largest lake in Africa, and the twelfth largest in the world. It is approximately 365 miles (787 kilometers) long and 52 miles (84 kilometers) wide at its

*Lake Malawi covers about one-fifth of Malawi's territory.*

widest point and it covers 8,900 square miles (23,051 square kilometers). It is one of the deepest lakes in Central Africa, reaching to a depth of 2,250 feet (686 meters).

Various travelers to Malawi have recorded their contradictory impressions of this lake, which is not only spectacularly beautiful, but possesses a sinister quality. One of the earliest and most well-known Western visitors to Malawi, Dr. David Livingstone, described the lake both as a lake of storms and as a lake of stars. Writing over one hundred years later, Oliver Ransford, a British government medical officer, described the lake both as, "an enchanted mirror tilted to reflect the languid artistry of the sky" and as, "an ugly woman scarred from all the cruelties of the past and grimacing with satisfaction at her curious ability not only to captivate men but to set them quarreling together."

Lake Malawi dominates the country's past and present. The first civilization known to have existed in Malawi, the Akafula society was centered on the shores of the lake. It was by the lake that the first Bantu people, the ancestors of the people that now inhabit the country, first settled. And it was the lake that gave the British their name for the colony that they formed on the western shore of the lake in 1891. The British called the country Nyasaland, the land of the lake (*nyasa* means "lake" in the local language). The lake was the setting for the horrors of the slave trade as many of the slaves were hauled across its waters to their fates in Mozambique or on the east coast. The slave traders set up their depots on its shores.

The lake is important in Malawi today. It provides fish for food and export, and makes transportation easy and relatively cheap. Its beautiful and varied scenery brings many tourists to the country, and the tourists in turn bring the foreign currency that is so important to Malawi's economic well-being. The lake's abundant waters are used to irrigate crops on the lakeshore, and, as they flow out through the Shire River, the lake's waters are used to create electricity. The lake, therefore, is a vital part of modern Malawian life.

When Malawi became independent from Britain in 1964, it adopted the name of the great Amaravi Confederation that had grown up on the lakeshore in the sixteenth century. (In Chichewa, the language of Malawi, *r* and *l* sound the same, and *w* is pronounced similar to *v*. Hence Maravi and Malawi are pronounced the same, although they are spelled differently.) The Amaravi were a Bantu group that migrated to the area as early as the thirteenth century. Their name, *Maravi*, means "flames" in the local language. There are many traditions explaining how the Amaravi got their name. One tradition says that the immigrants adopted the name when they came upon Lake Malawi that "shimmered like flames in the sunshine." Another tradition says the name was given to the immigrants because of their habit of setting the grass at the tops of hills on fire so that they would not lose touch with each other as they moved. Some say that the Amaravi brought fire to this region. Another explanation is that

the Amaravi were ironworkers who were known for their skill all over the area, and the name was given to them because of the fires in their ironworking furnaces.

Fire is still an important symbol in Malawi today. It is used as a symbol of personal transition and fires are built to mark important moments in the lives of ordinary people, such as the moment when a child becomes an adult. Fire is a national symbol. In the fight for independence from Britain, the president of Malawi, Dr. Hastings Kamuzu Banda, used to rally his followers by the cry of *kwacha*, which means "dawn." In this context, the fiery red of sunrise signified the dawning of a new day in Malawi's history, full of hope and energy. Malawi's struggle to make its dreams and hopes a reality is what gives Malawi its most distinctive character as a newly independent modern state.

*Chapter 2*

# A LAND OF CONTRASTS

---

There are three main types of landscape in Malawi: Rift valley, middleveld, and highveld. *Veld* is a South African word meaning "field." Only the Great Rift valley covers one continuous area. Areas of highveld and middleveld can be found scattered in different parts of the country, creating the great contrasts in relief that enhance Malawi's geographical variety and beauty.

## THE GREAT RIFT VALLEY

Malawi lies at the southern end of the Great East African Rift valley, which stretches southward down the eastern side of the African continent from the Red Sea in the north. The Rift valley has two branches: one runs through the Sudan and Uganda to the west of Lake Victoria, while the other goes through Kenya, on the east side of the lake. The two branches meet in Tanzania, just to the north of Malawi. The Rift valley was formed by parallel cracks in the earth's surface (called faults) that occurred thousands of years ago. All along the valley sides there are secondary cracks

*The Rift valley stretches the length of Malawi.*

that run perpendicular to the valley floor. Rivers flowing along these faults have eroded a number of spectacular gorges such as the Luweya River Gorge. One of the rivers running along a secondary fault forms the stunning Manchere Falls when it drops over one hundred feet (thirty meters) down a sheer cliff in a thin sheet of water.

The northern part of the Malawian Rift is occupied by Lake Malawi. The shores of Lake Malawi are characterized by a great variety of features, from the southern swamps to the wide plains that gradually rise to the middleveld and the steep escarpments in the north where the Ruarwe and Livingstone highlands border the lake. Lake Malawi has only one outlet, the Shire River. The Shire runs about 298 miles (480 kilometers) into the Zambezi River, one of Southern Africa's largest and most important waterways. After the Shire leaves Lake Malawi it flows slowly into Lake Malombe, only 5 miles (8 kilometers) away, and then into a flat floodplain where it meanders along in wide S-curves, creating a number of oxbow (U-shaped) lakes and bringing fertile soil to the area. Many people live on the banks of the Shire along this part of its course because the land is so fertile. After leaving the floodplain, the river becomes white as it descends rapidly through a series of potholes, rapids, and waterfalls. The most spectacular of these rapids and waterfalls are named Kholombidzo, Nkula, Tedzani, Matope, Kapachira, and Mpatamanga. The rapids make the middle course of the river impassable. The middle course of the river, nevertheless, is of great importance to Malawi. Hydroelectric plants have been built at Nkula and Tedzani falls to harness the power of the rushing water, and these provide cheap locally produced electricity for many areas in the country.

## THE MIDDLEVELD

The middleveld of Malawi includes all the land lying between roughly 2,000 and 4,000 feet (610 and 1,219 meters) above sea level. It mostly consists of gently sloping plains areas, and can be found along the lakeshore and between the highland areas. The largest area of middleveld relief includes the Kasungu and the Lilongwe plains that lie in the central region of Malawi. Mostly grasslands, these plains are characterized by numerous scattered shallow hollows in which rainwater collects to form seasonal ponds, marshes, or small lakes. The hollows are called *dambos*. Other middleveld areas include the Mzimba plain in the north and the Malombe plains at the southern end of Lake Malawi. Most of the middleveld plains are densely populated because they have fertile agricultural land.

There are two lakes in the middleveld named Chilwa and Chiuta. Lake Chilwa is an enclosed lake with no outlet. As is true of most lakes without an outlet, the waters of Lake Chilwa are slightly salty. The high rate of evaporation found in the area of the lake increases its saltiness. As the salts in the water have increased, the fish and other forms of life in the lake have begun to adapt, changing the chemistry of their bodies so that they can live in the salty water. Many studies are being done to record this unique process of evolution. Lake Chilwa is very shallow and it dried up completely in 1879 and nearly did so in 1968. Much of the lake's area is covered by swamps and reed beds.

Lake Chiuta, close to Lake Chilwa on the border of Mozambique, is a seasonal lake. It only holds water for half the year during the wet season. Lake Chiuta and Lake Chilwa were, at one time, one lake, but a sandbar gradually built up between them, creating two separate lakes.

## THE HIGHVELD

The highveld in Malawi consists of a series of widely separated plateaus and highlands. These areas contain some of the most spectacular scenery in the country. All the highland areas are relatively isolated and have a small population because of the difficulty of building roads up their steep slopes.

The highest mountains in Malawi are the Mulanje Mountains. The highest peak, Sapitwa, rises 9,843 feet (3,000 meters) above sea level—the highest point in Central Africa. The Mulanje Mountains rise sharply out of a plain in the southeast. In the spring,

Lake Malawi

Lilongwe ★

Lake Malombe

Lake Chiuta

Lake Chilwa

*Mud and thatch buildings belonging to farmers, with the Mulange Mountains in the background*

when smoke from bushfires makes the air hazy, Mulanje is almost hidden and the traveler will come upon it very suddenly as it rises straight up in unexpected splendor. In the wet season, the mountain's granite and green vegetation combine to give it a beautiful blue coloring when seen from a distance. The peaks of the mountain are often hidden in clouds or in the frequent mists.

*A village settlement in the Zomba Plateau*

A similar mountain lies to the northwest of Mulanje. Zomba Plateau rises 6,747 feet (2,087 meters) above sea level at its highest point. In the west, the mountain borders on the Rift valley and it drops sharply to the valley floor. The vegetation on the plateau is fairly dense. There are both planted and natural forests and the vegetation is green for most of the year because of the high rainfall that the plateau receives.

The largest highland area in Malawi is the beautiful northern

*Rolling hills of the Nyika Plateau*

Nyika Plateau. *Nyika* means "from where the water comes" and, indeed, the plateau forms the watershed for most of the northern region. Many of Malawi's rivers begin on its slopes. Like Zomba Plateau it borders on the Rift valley in the north and west, creating steep escarpments. The plateau itself consists of grass-covered, low rolling hills that stretch as far as the eye can see. The landscape has been compared to that of the Scottish Highlands. Not far away is the Ruarwe Scarp, which plunges 5,000 feet (1,524 meters) into Lake Malawi. The highland above the scarp is distinguished by the pulpwood pine forest plantation that covers a large part of its upper slopes.

## CLIMATE

Malawi lies within the tropics and has a generally mild climate. The temperate climate makes a fairly simple life-style possible because the temperature rarely reaches extremes of hot or cold. Houses therefore can be constructed out of natural materials, like mud bricks and grass thatching because there is no need to keep out uncomfortable weather. Clothing tends to be fairly simple for the same reason, usually consisting of cotton cloths wrapped around the body in various ways.

The climatic year in Malawi cannot be divided easily into consecutive seasons such as spring, summer, autumn, and winter. Instead, there are two seasons which overlap one another. The hot, wet season, when Malawi comes under the influence of monsoon winds from the Indian Ocean, lasts from October to April. The rest of the year is relatively cold and dry. Because Malawi lies in the Southern Hemisphere, the coldest months of the year are April, May, June, and July. During this period, the temperature can fall under 50 degrees Fahrenheit (10 degrees Celsius) during the night. The sun shines almost every day during these months and the daily temperature usually lies in the mid-60s degrees Fahrenheit (about 18 degrees Celsius). The hottest month of the year, and the most uncomfortable, is October when both the humidity and the temperature rise. Although October is the hottest month, the hot season in Malawi usually lasts until March.

Malawi has two unique features that characterize its climate.

*Malawi has a great variety of vegetation—from grasslands (left) to woodlands (right).*

One is called the *chiperoni*. It is so-called because it is a wind that brings a cool, misty drizzle from the direction of Mt. Chiperoni in Mozambique. This kind of weather occurs most often in the Shire Highlands during the cold season, and it usually lasts about three days. The other unique feature of Malawi's climate is the *mvera*, a strong, gusting southeast wind that can whip the lake up into waves that are 10 feet (3 meters) high, and can blow over huge trees on the lakeshore.

## VEGETATION

Given the diversity of relief and climate that characterizes Malawi, it is not surprising that the country has a great variety of vegetation, ranging from open grasslands in the low-lying plains, to thorn scrub on the southern lakeshore, to woodlands and dense forests. Approximately one-quarter of the country is covered by forest. Typical trees include the green mopane; the fan palms that surround the lake; mchenga trees which, like mopane, shed their leaves to withstand the drought of the dry season; the msasa, which can grow over fifty-nine feet (eighteen meters) tall if the soil is deep; and the mukwa, which is used for making furniture. The most common type of vegetation is the indigenous brachystegia forest, which covers the escarpment slopes of Malawi. The brachystegia are distinctive because their new leaves are deep red and gold, later turning bright green, and then, finally, a very dark green. When the early morning sun catches a hillside of new leaves, the forest can look like it is on fire. Remnants of the indigenous hardwood evergreen forests, with their mahogany and pencil cedars, also can still be found, mostly in the highveld areas of Malawi.

Malawi has a number of interesting tree species. The Mlanje cedar tree, with its heavily sweet-scented gold wood, grows only on the slopes of the Mulanje Mountains and Zomba and Nyika plateaus. A soft wood, the Mlanje cedar is a favorite among craft workers who fashion various articles out of it. Especially beautiful are the cedar boxes, which come in different sizes and are carved in geometric designs that complement the wood's natural grain. The "umbrella" tree is another tree that grows in the highveld areas. The leaves of this tree form a series of flat, green canopies parallel to each other and to the ground. The trees often are seen perched precariously on steep slopes, and they are usually covered in lichens, mosses, and creepers. The immense, pink-gray, awkward baobab is found mostly in the low-lying areas around the lakeshore and in the Shire valley. The baobab looks like a tree that has grown upside down with its roots in the air. The tree provides a hard fruit which, when cracked open, yields seeds covered with a thirst-quenching substance that tastes

*Left: The fruit of the sausage tree   Right: A baobab tree*

somewhat like cream of tartar. Growing in the same areas as the
baobab is the "sausage" tree, with its sausage-shaped fruit. These
fruit are extremely heavy and hard. It is said that if one of them
fell from high enough, it could kill an elephant.

## WILDLIFE

Malawi used to have a great many wild animals. Today, wildlife
usually can be seen only in the country's relatively extensive
protected areas such as Nyika Plateau, Viphya Plateau, and Vwaza
Marsh in the north; Kasungu National Park and Nkhota Kota
Game Reserve in the central region; and the Lake Malawi
National Park, Liwonde Game Reserve, Lengwe National Park,
and Elephant March in the south.

One of the most common wild animal found in Malawi is the
antelope. There are many species of antelope in Malawi ranging

*Kasungu National Park*

from the black sable, with its graceful horns that curve over its back; through the kudu, with its huge horns that are curved like a corkscrew; to the tiny suni, a brownish-gray antelope the size of a rabbit with straight sharp horns. Suni are so small that they are easy prey for hungry African pythons. The shy and rare nyala antelope can be seen in Lengwe National Park, while the stately brick-colored roan antelope is often seen on the Nyika Plateau.

Some of the many varieties
of antelopes found
in Malawi are sables (top),
impalas (above left),
and kudus (right).

Clockwise from top left: A black rhino,
an olive baboon, a pair of zebras,
and hippopotamuses

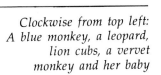

*Clockwise from top left:*
*A blue monkey, a leopard,*
*lion cubs, a vervet*
*monkey and her baby*

In addition to antelope, elephants, black rhinos, hippos, buffalo, and zebras can be seen, and lions, leopards, and some smaller wildcats have been sighted in most of the protected areas. The baboon, with its long face and huge jaws, is a common sight, as is the playful vervet monkey. A careful observer might catch a glimpse of the rare samango or blue monkey, although they are often confused with the vervet.

*A majestic African elephant (left)
and African buffalo (above)*

    These animals are not the only type of wildlife found in
Malawi. The country has more than six hundred species of birds.
Of these, one of the most striking is the majestic fish eagle, which
is common on the lakeshore. The fish eagle resembles the
American bald eagle, with its white head and dark body. The
underside of its wings are rust brown and its tail is white. It has a
distinctive piercing cry, which it produces while throwing back its
head. Another spectacular bird is the carmine bee-eater, which
lives in colonies on riverbanks. As its name suggests, this bird is a
deep pink, with turquoise on its head and rump. It catches insects

*The fish eagle (top left),*
*carmine bee-eaters (above),*
*and a lilac-breasted roller (left)*

in the air while turning and twisting gracefully, and it is beautiful to watch. The lilac-breasted roller is another striking bird, with bright turquoise wings and tail and a lovely lilac breast. The roller gets its name from its "loop the loop" mating display flight. Livingstone's lourie is a big bird, about the size of a crow. It is bright leaf green, with a face and crest that are streaked with white. On the underside of its wings, clearly seen when it flies, it has a striking red patch. The lourie's cry is very harsh. Apart from these birds, Malawi has a number of unique or rare species such as the striking bar-tailed trogon, the vanga flycatcher, and sharpe's akalat.

*A large variety of brilliantly colored butterflies are found in Malawi.*

Malawi has an enormous number of lovely butterflies of which the most striking is the pearl charaxes, a fairly large butterfly covered in luminous scales that appear white, pink, or green depending on how they catch the light. The green-banded swallowtail is another beautiful butterfly. It is jet black with one iridescent blue-green stripe on the upper side of its wings. The blue pansy is striking because of the large bright blue spots on its back wings, while the gaudy commodore is interesting because it has two very different forms. During the wet season, the commodore is predominantly red, while during the dry season the butterfly is mostly a violet blue with red spots. Both forms have black streaks on their wings.

*Tourist accommodations in Kasungu National Park*

Malawi's wildlife and vegetation form one of the country's most valuable resources. Protecting those resources is a high priority for the Malawian government. Over 10 percent of the country's land is protected in game and nature reserves, one of the highest percentages in Africa. Both wildlife and vegetation are being threatened by the growing number of people who cut down the forests for firewood, and destroy the wild habitats where the animals live. One of the most difficult problems Malawi will face in the future is to find a balance between providing enough land and food for its people and protecting its natural resources.

*Looking east across Lake Malawi to Mozambique*

# Chapter 3

# THE RISE AND FALL
## OF THE AMARAVI
### FEDERATION

---

## THE BANTU

The people of present-day Malawi are part of a large family of African people called the Bantu. The word *bantu* means "people." This word is found in all the related languages of the group. It is thought that the Bantu originally came from the Congo Basin (to the west of Malawi). Sometime before the beginning of A.D., the Bantu began to increase in numbers and to move outward from their central homeland. By A.D. 200 they had spread into Malawi and as far as the East African coast, and by 400 some had traveled as far south as modern South Africa. As the Bantu settled in different regions, they split into many different groups. Each group developed its own language and culture that was similar and yet distinct.

The Bantu people were farmers. They grew crops and raised cattle. They were skilled in the techniques of metalworking, which they introduced into the indigenous communities where they settled. Many of the areas into which the Bantu moved were

*When the Bantu moved into Malawi, they found a pigmy group living in the area.*

inhabited by people who were not farmers, but who lived by hunting and gathering wild vegetation. The Bantu, with their relatively settled way of life and their large communities, brought many changes into these areas.

## THE AKAFULA

The Bantu who spread into Malawi found the area occupied by a pygmy group called the Akafula. The Akafula lived on the western lakeshore in small communities that periodically moved around the lake. They had no settled villages. While the men fished and hunted for food, the women gathered wild roots, berries, and leaves to eat. For the most part, the Bantu groups settled in peace near the Akafula. Gradually, the Akafula began to adopt the farming techniques of their Bantu neighbors. The population of the area began to increase as the Bantu and Akafula grew prosperous. Akafula began to marry Bantu and people began to live in larger and larger communities. As the size of the population and communities increased, it became necessary to develop some kind of government, and a system of ruling chiefs emerged.

## THE AMARAVI

The modern republic of Malawi takes its name from a powerful grouping of people that emerged around 1400 on the shores of Lake Malawi. This group was called the Amaravi. The Amaravi, or the Malawi, were made up of a number of different people who spoke the same language, Nyanja. Their ancestors were Bantu who came from the northwest and intermarried with the Akafula and other Bantu groups who had settled in the area in earlier times. From these roots a new people arose with distinctive traditions and customs. One of the traditions that developed among the Amaravi was that of a dual power system. The Bantu groups who migrated into the area of Lake Malawi brought with them a system of government by chiefs. But those who held power among the earlier inhabitants of the area were the religious leaders who were believed to ensure the good harvests so essential to the survival of the community.

Since they were not able to establish their rule over the local population by force, the incoming Bantu chiefs compromised. They allowed the local religious leaders to retain much of their traditional ritual functions and powers, but they took over such political duties as leading the army, controlling trade and foreign relations, and establishing law and order. Gradually, as the immigrants intermarried with the local population, some Bantu groups began to take over the religious leadership. The division of power remained, but it was no longer between indigenous and immigrant groups. Instead the division was between two Bantu groups. The Phiri clan, a later immigrant group, provided the chiefs for the Amaravi, while the Banda clan, who had been living on the land longer, provided the powerful priests.

By 1500 there were a number of different Amaravi chieftainships around Lake Malawi, including that of Karonga, Undi, Nkanda, and Mwase. Much of their power and influence in the area came from their involvement in the profitable ivory trade with the East African coast. Although these chieftainships cooperated in matters of trade, and their chiefs were related to each other by blood and marriage, by the beginning of the sixteenth century they had not yet formed any political union or federation. As trade increased, the power of certain chiefs increased, and they began to expand their areas of influence and establish their rule over other chiefs who had not been as successful in the ivory trade.

The more powerful chiefs were given the title *kalonga*. By 1600 a few kalonga had managed to establish power over huge areas around Lake Malawi. The most powerful kalonga was Mzura. Mzura was able to extend his power in all directions by conquering weaker chiefs and by making alliances with those he could not conquer. By the end of Mzura's reign, Amaravi overlordship was recognized throughout most of the lands between the Shire River and the Indian Ocean to the east. Mzura was strong enough to make peace with his greatest rivals at this time, the Portuguese, who were expanding rapidly from the east coast in search of gold, ivory, and slaves. Many African chieftainships were conquered by the Portuguese during this period, but Mzura remained independent and dealt with the Portuguese as an equal power.

Mzura's reign brought a period of peace and prosperity to the area around Lake Malawi, and the land between the lake and the east coast. After his death, his empire gradually fell apart. This was partly because Mzura's power was personal. People were loyal to Mzura because he was a wise and strong leader, but there was no structure or central government that could hold the empire together in his absence. Various chiefs who had owed their allegiance to Mzura rebelled against his successors who were neither as powerful nor as skilled in government. One of the strongest groups to break away from the Amaravi Confederation was led by Undi. Undi (which was both the title of the chief and his name) was able to build up considerable power on his own, and by 1700 the Portuguese referred to him as the king of Maravi. Undi's empire was never as large as Mzura's, and by the end of the eighteenth century it had fallen apart in the same way. In 1831-32, a Portuguese explorer named A.C.P. Gamitto recorded that no empire existed in Malawi: "all these peoples today are totally independent of each other," he wrote.

## THE SLAVE TRADE

The nineteenth century was a time of trouble. It was during this period that the slave trade reached Malawi. The East African slave trade had begun in the eighth century when Muslim traders from the lands of the Middle East moved down the east coast of Africa

*Slaves, in chains and yokes, were taken to be sold.*

and set up trading posts in what are now Kenya, Tanzania, and Mozambique. At that time, the Arabs mostly traded in ivory, gold, and cloth, and the slave trade was relatively insignificant. The Arabs gradually began to penetrate into the interior of Africa in search of new things to trade. In the twelfth century one of their sailboats was blown into the mouth of the Zambezi River, which penetrates deep into the Southern African interior and is linked to Lake Malawi by the Shire River. This discovery made the Arab expansion easier and faster. By the sixteenth century, the profits from the ivory and gold trade were decreasing, and the Arabs began to trade in human labor in the form of slaves.

Until the eighteenth century, the slave trade was not large enough to force the Arabs to raid for slaves beyond the coastal areas over which they had control. In the eighteenth century, the Arabs began to find themselves in heavy competition with the Portuguese for slaves, ivory, and gold. The Arabs then began to expand farther and farther inland in their search for slaves. They

*An Arab slave ship*

found a rich source of slaves in the area around Lake Malawi where the Amaravi Confederation was disintegrating and the chiefs were too weak or too busy fighting among themselves to protect their people from slave raids. By the end of the eighteenth century, Lake Malawi was one of the strongest centers of the slave trade in East Africa.

The slaves who were taken in raids were rounded up and marched in pairs to the coast. Each slave was attached to another slave by a heavy wooden yoke, called a *goli*, that rested on the shoulders, much like the yoke used to control cattle. Each pair of slaves was then chained to other pairs by their hands or feet, or sometimes by the neck. They were forced to march to the lake carrying ivory or other goods that also were to be traded. They were then transported across the lake in Arab boats (called *dhows*) and marched to the coast, or sold to plantation owners in Mozambique, Mombasa, or Zanzibar. Many slaves died on the journey.

*Slaves who were too weak to march to the coast were left to die.*

The slave trade was disastrous for Malawi. The people who raided for slaves were ruthless and cruel. They burned villages and crops and murdered many of those whom they did not take to sell. Numerous areas were devastated and depopulated. People lived in constant fear. As a result of slave raids, many villages contained only old people and children who could not be sold for a profit. There was no one to plow the fields and plant crops, so there was a great deal of famine. This was a very dark period in Malawi's history.

The disintegration of the Amaravi Confederation was not the only reason for the ease with which the Arabs were able to take slaves from the area around Lake Malawi. Part of the reason for the tremendous expansion of the slave trade in Malawi was the rise of a number of groups who wanted to gain power and were willing to do so by selling people, either those they had captured in raids or their own people. One of the most prominent of these groups was the Yao.

The Yao originally lived to the east of the lake and until the 1850s they were not unified. In the 1850s four groups of Yao moved across the lake into southern Malawi. Skilled in warfare and trade, the Yao began to take control of the slave trade and part of the ivory trade. By the late nineteenth century, the Yao were the strongest group in Malawi.

Another group whose power depended on the slave trade, although to a much smaller extent than the Yao, were the Tumbuka. They lived mostly around the northern part of Lake Malawi. Around 1800 they were united in a confederation by Chikulamayembe, who was a skilled trader. Although the Tumbuka traded some slaves, they mostly traded in ivory, and they successfully challenged Amaravi control of the northern trade routes to the east coast. As their wealth grew, so did their power.

Another group of people associated with the slave trade rose to power in Malawi. These were Swahili traders from the east coast who settled on the lakeshore and took control of much of the slave trade across Lake Malawi. The most well known of these traders was Jumbe, who established a settlement at Nkhota Kota on the western shore of the lake. Nkhota Kota, which became one of the largest villages in Central Africa, was a slave-trading settlement. Today, the paths where the slaves were marched still exist. They are broad, well-kept paths, lined on either side by the tall kapok tree with its distinctive horizontal branches.

## THE ARRIVAL OF OUTSIDE FORCES

The land of the lake was not only disrupted by the activities of newly powerful groups in the area. At the same time as the Yao and the Tumbuka were becoming powerful, other foreign groups began to enter the region. One of these groups came from the south. The end of the eighteenth century in South Africa was marked by numerous wars between the Zulu and other African people. Many fled, among them the Ngoni who moved northward in 1835 under Zwagendaba. After Zwagendaba's death in 1845, the Ngoni split up into a number of different groups who carved out little states all over the region. Although the Ngoni did not sell slaves to Arab and Portuguese traders, they did raid villages and take captives to work in their own fields. These captives were better off in some ways than those sold to outside traders, because they were eventually incorporated into the society as family members. But the raiding for slaves was very disruptive to the societies that existed around Lake Malawi.

Another new force in Malawian life came from the far north. On September 17, 1859, Dr. David Livingstone, the famous Scottish medical missionary and explorer, reached Lake Malawi (or Lake Nyasa as it was called then). He is credited with being the first European in Malawi, although some Portuguese explorers are known to have reached the lake earlier. Livingstone's visit was certainly the most publicized, and it was his writing that brought knowledge of the lake and the people who lived on its shores to many Europeans.

David Livingstone was born in 1813 in Blantyre, a small industrial town near Glasgow in Scotland. Livingstone's family was poor and he spent long hours working in a cotton mill to save enough money for medical school. Having wanted to be a missionary since he was a child, Livingstone left for South Africa soon after he received his qualifications as a doctor. He worked there for over ten years. It was during this time that he first heard of the forested country that lay to the north of the Kalahari Desert and the great river that watered it. Livingstone was determined to find and explore this land. In 1849 he made his first expedition

*David Livingstone (right) and his boyhood home (left)*

across the desert, and in 1851, on a second expedition, he met a king whose land lay on the fabled Zambezi River. He heard many stories about the cruelties of the slave trade in Central Africa.

Livingstone believed that if a profitable trade in things other than people could be developed in Central Africa, the slave trade would be destroyed. He convinced the London Missionary Society to allow him to explore Central Africa and discover what could be traded. Between 1852 and 1856 Livingstone traveled from South Africa to the southwest coast of Africa and then across the continent to Mozambique on the east coast. It was a journey of over 4,000 miles (6,437 kilometers), made almost entirely on foot. Everywhere Livingstone went he made maps and took notes on the people he met and on the horrors of the slave trade. Upon his return to England he published his notes in a book called *Missionary Travels and Researches in South Africa*. It became a best-

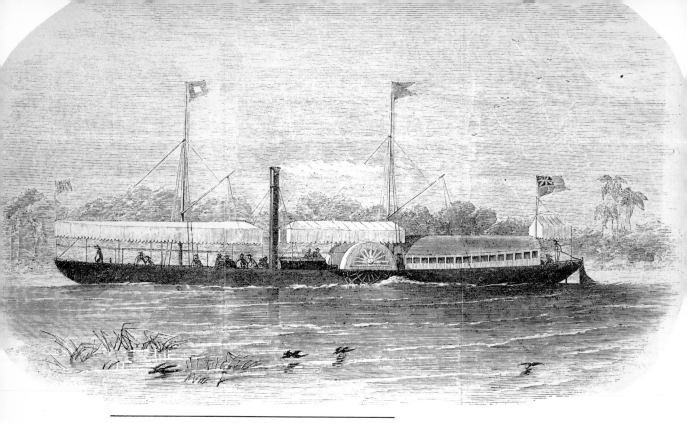

*The steamer Dr. Livingstone used in his explorations*

seller and Livingstone was invited to speak all over Britain. He
was at the center of a rising hostility to the slave trade, and the
growing humanitarian determination to end it. In 1858 the British
government agreed to sponsor an expedition into Central Africa
along the Zambezi River to suppress the slave trade, open
missions, and develop communication links for trade.

It was on the Zambezi Expedition that Dr. Livingstone traveled
up the Shire River, into the Shire Highlands, onward to Lake
Chilwa and then, finally, to the great Lake Malawi itself. In 1861,
when Bishop Charles Mackenzie and some other missionaries
from the Universities' Mission to Central Africa (UMCA) were
sent to Africa, Livingstone led them up the Shire River into
Malawi, where they established the country's first mission station
at Magomero in the Shire valley. Livingstone hoped that his
mission would be the first step to bringing Christianity to the

*Livingstone's body was carried thousands of miles to the coast by his faithful African porters and then shipped to England.*

natives of Malawi and ending the slave trade. But by 1863, Livingstone's dreams had been shattered. The Magomero mission had failed because of tension between the missionaries and the powerful slave traders. Bishop Mackenzie and several missionaries died from fever. The British government withdrew its support from the Zambezi Expedition because of its failure to stop the slave trade in the region and because of the tension that had developed between Livingstone, embittered by the death of his wife in 1862, and the members of the expedition.

Livingstone died in Zambia on another journey to the African interior in 1873. His body was carried thousands of miles to the coast by his faithful African porters and taken by ship to England where he was buried. Although he did not live to see the end of the slave trade, Livingstone's efforts had made Africa known to Europe. His love of the land and the people came through in his

*The cathedral on Likoma Island in the middle of Lake Malawi*

writing and gave a small number of Europeans a new respect for Africa. Livingstone's works brought about a turning point in the relationship between Africa and Europe. After his death, Europeans became more and more involved in African affairs.

Three new missions were established in Malawi alone. In 1875 a Free Church of Scotland mission was established at Cape Maclear as a memorial to Livingstone's achievements. Although many of the original missionaries died of fever, and the mission needed to be moved first north to Bandawe and then north again into the mountains that had been named for Livingstone, the Livingstonia Mission still stands today, and many leaders from all over Southern Africa were educated in its school. Another Church of Scotland mission was established in the Shire Highlands. Led by the Reverend Henry Henderson, the mission was named Blantyre after Livingstone's birthplace. One of the missionaries, Reverend D.C.R. Scott, and a group of local craftsmen built the Church of St.

Michael and All Angels. The church was designed by Scott, who had no formal training in architecture. Scott would simply have the workmen lay out the bricks, and if he were satisfied with how they looked he would have them add mortar. Each brick was made on the site in one of eighty-one different hand-carved molds. The church still stands today—one of the oldest buildings in Malawi.

The Free Church of Scotland was not alone in sending out missionaries. In 1882 UMCA sent out two Anglican bishops who established a mission center on Likoma Island in the middle of Lake Malawi. From this base, the Anglicans established many missions around the lake, traveling in ships owned by the missions. One of the missionaries at Likoma, Will Johnson, later helped build a beautiful brick cathedral on the island. Another famous missionary, Chauncy Maples, was later made bishop of the new diocese but he drowned soon after he arrived when his boat capsized on the lake.

Although the missionaries were the first Europeans to settle in Malawi, others followed. In 1878 a group of Scottish businessmen formed the Livingstonia Central Africa Company to develop trade in the area and supply the missionaries with the things they needed. They placed their headquarters near the Blantyre Mission in the Shire Highlands under the management of the Moir brothers. This company, later called the African Lakes Company and then the African Lakes Corporation, was fairly successful in opening up trade in the area, and it remained important in Malawi for many years. However, during its early years, it was unable to do anything about ending the slave trade. It would take a series of wars against the slave raiders, and the involvement of many more Europeans to accomplish that.

*Many British imperialists dreamed of controlling the area around Lake Malawi.*

# Chapter 4

# COLONIALISM, NATIONALISM, AND INDEPENDENCE

During the early and middle parts of the nineteenth century, the British were able to trade and preach in the area around Lake Malawi without taking control. In the late 1800s this situation changed because of competition from other European powers, not only in Malawi, but in other parts of Africa and the world. In 1884 the European powers held a conference in Berlin where they insisted that the powers would have to establish their authority in regions where they wanted to have an influence. The British wished to secure their trade and missions in Southern and Central Africa, especially along the Zambezi River where they faced great competition from the Portuguese. Since the Shire River flowed into the Zambezi, Malawi was very important to the British. The area around Lake Malawi was important because it lay in the middle of the great colonial empire that many British imperialists dreamed of—stretching from Cape Town in South Africa to Cairo in Egypt. Therefore the British were anxious to establish their control over the area. They were given an added excuse by the wars that broke out around the lake in the last part of the nineteenth century.

In 1884 the African Lakes Corporation decided to expand into the north of what is now Malawi—into the peaceful land of the Ngonde. They sent Montieth Fotheringham, a Scotsman who was an agent of the corporation, to establish a trading post at Karonga. Conflict arose between the traders and Mlozi, an infamous outlaw who was half-Arab and half-Malawian. Mlozi led a well-armed gang of slave raiders and in 1886 he moved into the land of the Ngonde. Mlozi enslaved many of the Ngonde and massacred those who could not be enslaved. Fotheringham was outraged and he declared war on Mlozi. It was a war that would take the British many years to win. In 1888, Captain Frederick Lugard (who later became a famous British colonialist and a lord) arrived to lead the battle. By this time Mlozi had built himself a strong fort, and despite repeated attacks and the aid of a cannon that was dragged from Karonga, Lugard and his forces were unable to defeat him. Lugard returned to England in 1889, leaving Fotheringham to continue the war on his own.

The British government did not totally desert Fotheringham. In 1891 they declared a protectorate over the area. At first the area was called the Nyasaland Districts, but its name was later changed to the British Central African Protectorate. Although the protectorate was officially established only to protect the people who lived around Lake Malawi, it gave firm control of the area to the British government for the next seventy years.

The government appointed Sir Harry Hamilton Johnston as colonial commissioner for the new protectorate. Sir Harry spent much of his time in expanding the area of British rule in Malawi, ending the wars of resistance, and trying to stop the slave trade. In

*Sir Harry Hamilton Johnston (left) helped to stop the slave trade. Tea gardens (right) near Blantyre*

1895 Sir Harry defeated Jumbe and forced him to leave Nkhota Kota, which then became part of the protectorate. Earlier Sir Harry had tried to end the war between the African Lakes Corporation and Mlozi. He signed a peace treaty with Mlozi agreeing not to interfere with his slave raids if Mlozi would agree not to attack Fotheringham or his traders. During the period of fragile peace that followed this treaty, Mlozi grew more and more powerful. When Fotheringham died of fever in 1895, Mlozi refused to renew the treaty. Sir Harry, who had built up a small army by this time, sent a strong force to attack Mlozi. After heavy bombardment of his fortress, Mlozi was forced to flee. He was captured and executed. After his death the slave trade in Malawi began to decrease.

Sir Harry Johnston was able to do a great deal to stop the slave trade in Malawi. He was able to suppress opposition to the British government's takeover. Under his rule, the area became relatively peaceful. The peace attracted other Europeans. Some came to farm and they built huge plantations of coffee, cotton, tobacco, and tea out of the lands previously held by Africans. Others came as government agents. This group increased after 1907 when the protectorate was confirmed and renamed the British Protectorate of Nyasaland.

## NYASALAND

Nyasaland was different from the other British colonies in Southern Africa. Economic development in Nyasaland was slower than in the other British colonies in the region, especially Southern Rhodesia. This was partly because, while Southern Rhodesia had gold, coal, and diamonds, and Northern Rhodesia had copper, Nyasaland had no minerals at all. Therefore, industrial development was very slow. In addition, Nyasaland was not linked to the coast by rail until 1935, so it was difficult to export and import goods. When the railway to the coast was completed, the protectorate began to grow at a faster rate. The economic recovery was helped by the development of tea estates in the south.

Another reason for the protectorate's delayed development was that European immigration, although encouraged by the British government, was slower to Nyasaland than to its richer neighbors. Large blocks of land were sold, leased, or given to Europeans, but most of the land was reserved for Africans. This was very unusual. In Southern Rhodesia and South Africa, the Africans were pushed into smaller and smaller areas, and the white Europeans were given most of the land. Even in Nyasaland, European agriculture dominated the economy. Short on funds and under pressure from farmers who were having difficulty getting workers for their farms, the government gave support to planters who used the hated "tangata system." This was a system whereby Africans were allowed to remain on the land and work on their own farms provided that they worked on the European farms for at least one month of the year. There were many abuses of this system with European farmers and plantation owners requiring more and more work on their farms. High taxes made the system very unprofitable for the African farmers and many had to leave their land. This was one of the causes for the discontent that led to the Chilembwe Uprising.

Since Nyasaland was under British rule, its people were required to defend Britain in its conflicts with other nations. Malawians fought in both World Wars. In World War I Nyasaland became an important British and Allied base. Lake Malawi was the site of the first naval engagement of World War I when the only British gunboat on the lake, H.M.S. *Gwendolen*, was sent to destroy the German gunboat, *Hermann von Wissman*. The German boat was, in fact, captured in a bloodless battle.

The British organized the Malawians into one of the regiments of the King's African Rifles, the KAR. British and Malawian troops clashed with and defeated the Germans (who had a colony just to the north of the lake) at the Battle of Kasowa on the Ngonde Plain. In addition, many Malawians in the KAR were sent to other parts of East Africa to help fight against the Germans. In World War II, thirty thousand Malawians served Britain and the Allies. They distinguished themselves in battle in East and North Africa, as well as in such faraway places as Madagascar and Burma.

In 1953 the British government created the Central African Federation. The federation was composed of the Nyasaland Protectorate (now Malawi), Northern Rhodesia (now Zambia), and Southern Rhodesia (now Zimbabwe). The reasons for the union of these three British territories were many, and they were different for each of the governments involved. The British government was concerned about the repressive racial policies of the Southern Rhodesian white settler government, and they hoped that the more liberal governments of Northern Rhodesia and Nyasaland would keep white Rhodesian racism in check. It was believed that the union would economically benefit all three colonies. Nyasaland especially could benefit from the more advanced industrial development of Northern and Southern Rhodesia.

The Southern Rhodesian politicians who wanted the federation saw things in a different way. They thought that they would be able to dominate the federation and therefore gain more power over the region. They believed they would be able to gain wealth from copper mines of Northern Rhodesia, and they saw Nyasaland as providing the labor that they so desperately needed for their mines and farms. In fact, the Southern Rhodesian settlers had the most realistic view. The Central African Federation is seen by most historians as having had a negative economic and political effect on both Northern Rhodesia and Nyasaland. The people who gained the most were the white settlers of Southern Rhodesia.

## THE CHILEMBWE UPRISING

The imposition of British colonial rule on Malawi was not welcomed by all. Many Africans resisted the expansion of European control and the destruction of their own political and social systems. Throughout the twentieth century there were

*Booker T. Washington was one of the people who influenced Reverend John Chilembwe.*

outbreaks of unrest in the African communities. In the first part of the century, much of the protest came from the Africans' local churches.

One of the first serious uprisings against British colonial rule in Malawi was led by the Reverend John Chilembwe. Chilembwe was a Yao minister who had been converted by Joseph Booth, a radical independent British missionary traveling alone in Africa. Booth sent Chilembwe to attend a seminary in the United States. Chilembwe was graduated in 1900 and returned home to form his own mission in southern Nyasaland. It was called the Providence Industrial Mission. It expanded rapidly, especially in the area around Blantyre, and many churches and schools were built. The mission's concern for its people brought many converts.

Chilembwe was influenced by such humanitarian Afro-American leaders as Booker T. Washington. Chilembwe preached a message that was openly critical of the British government in Malawi. His radicalism brought many converts to his church. Africans were discontent because of rising prices and increased taxes. They were angry at new laws that undermined traditional authority and increased British control.

Tension between the mission and the British government and their settler supporters increased. When some of Chilembwe's churches were burned by white settlers, Chilembwe and his followers rebelled. On January 23, 1915, they attacked the Magomero estate near the Mulanje Mountains, killing three European estate officers. The revolt lasted two weeks, until British forces were brought in from the north to help put it down. Chilembwe was shot and a number of other leaders were imprisoned or executed. The Europeans were terrified and believed the African rebels would kill them all. Despite the initial killings of three Europeans, Chilembwe and his followers were remarkably anxious to treat European women and children well and the slaughter that was expected never took place.

## AFRICAN NATIONALISM AND INDEPENDENCE

Although the British administration in the Nyasaland Protectorate was known for its comparatively liberal policies toward Africans, the Malawian people never stopped longing for independence. They found the limits that colonial rule placed on their actions and lives increasingly frustrating. They had no influence in the way that their country was governed and they could not rise above a certain level in their jobs, although they had the skills to do so. They were looked down upon by the Europeans. Their frustration was made worse by fear when the Southern Rhodesian white settlers began to pressure the British government into creating a federation. The African nationalists feared that the white settlers would gain more power and extend their oppressive racial policies into Nyasaland. They believed that under Southern Rhodesian influence they would lose their chance

*Africans in Blantyre at a rally for independence*

of self-rule. After the Central African Federation was created in 1953, African nationalism grew rapidly in Nyasaland.

The first openly political organization for Africans in Malawi was the Nyasaland Congress party—the NCP. It was formed in 1944 to represent the Malawian people. The NCP spread quickly. Branches were organized throughout the country in cooperation with the traditional Malawian leaders—the chiefs. The NCP demanded representation in government and the expansion of education for Africans. When these demands were rejected by the British administration, the NCP began to struggle for full independence. In 1958, the NCP called for the return of Dr. Banda, a leader whom the people called the *Ngwazi* (the "hero"), to form a national movement in Nyasaland. In July of that year, Dr. Banda arrived in Blantyre to lead the Nyasaland African Congress.

Hastings Banda was born in 1898 in Kasungu, which lies in Malwai's Central Province. He was named Kamuzu, meaning "little root." While still young, he developed a thirst for knowledge. He first went to school at the Church of Scotland

*Dr. Hastings Kamuzu Banda became president for life in 1971.*

Mission at Kasungu. When he was thirteen Banda walked more than 1,000 miles (1,609 kilometers) to South Africa in search of educational opportunities. On his journey he worked whenever he could to pay his own way. He was employed as a hospital orderly in what is now Zimbabwe, and then as a laborer, a clerk, and an interpreter in the gold mines of South Africa. Hastings Banda stayed in South Africa for eight years, slowly saving enough money to go to medical school. He was awarded a scholarship to study in the United States, where he earned a degree in philosophy from the University of Chicago and a medical degree from Meharry Medical College in Tennessee. After completing his qualifications as a doctor in 1937, Dr. Banda went to Britain where he attended the Edinburgh medical school. He then built up a successful medical practice first in Liverpool, then in North Shields, and finally in London.

Throughout his career Dr. Banda remained dedicated to his homeland. While he was in London he kept in touch with many of his fellow Malawians and he shared his ideals about Africa with a number of famous African leaders such as Jomo Kenyatta of Kenya and Kwame Nkrumah of Ghana. He consulted with the nationalist leaders in Nyasaland. Dr. Banda strongly opposed the Central African Federation and when it was created in 1953, he left England and went to Ghana to serve the sick there. He returned to Malawi in 1958 when he took over the leadership of the Nyasaland African Congress. In December 1958 he attended the first Pan-African Congress in Ghana and met with many African leaders. When he returned to Malawi, he brought with him a new era of freedom.

After Dr. Banda's return to Malawi, the tension between the administration and the African people rose. In January 1959, at a meeting of the African Congress (which Dr. Banda did not attend), there were threats that a campaign of violence against the whites was planned. During February there were some isolated incidents of violence against property and in March the British administration declared a state of emergency. The Nyasaland African Congress was banned and its leaders, including Dr. Banda, were herded up and imprisoned. Many others were arrested too. At a meeting in Nkhata Bay, twenty Africans were killed trying to avoid arrest.

Opposition to the federation kept increasing and the British government began to realize that, without the support of the majority of the African population in the three territories, the federation could not survive. In 1960, Dr. Banda was released. He formed the Malawi Congress party, which won a tremendous victory in the general elections that took place in 1961 under a

*In 1959 the British declared a state of emergency in Malawi and troops were brought out.*

newly written constitution. Thousands of Malawians walked, some as many as ten miles (sixteen kilometers), to the polling booths to put their mark next to the black rooster, the Congress party's symbol. Once the Congress party had won, they demanded that Nyasaland be allowed to leave the federation and regain full independence.

On February 1, 1963, Nyasaland was granted internal self-government and Dr. Banda was elected prime minister. The Central African Federation was officially dissolved in December of the same year. On July 6, 1964, the country became fully independent and was renamed Malawi. In 1966, the country was declared a republic within the British Commonwealth, and Dr. Hastings Kamuzu Banda became its first president. In 1971, Dr. Banda became president for life.

Supporters of Dr. Banda and the Malawi Congress party carry a
casket symbolizing the death of federation (above) while they
wait for Dr. Banda to be sworn in as president (below).

*Government offices in Lilongwe*

# Chapter 5

# *THE MODERN REPUBLIC*

---

The people of Malawi have traveled a long way through time since their ancestors hunted on the shores of the great lake. A number of things distinguish modern Malawi from the earlier societies that existed in the area. One of the characteristics that makes modern Malawi different is its system of government.

## GOVERNMENT

Modern Malawi is a one-party state. The only party that exists in the country is the Malawi Congress party (MCP) that swept the elections in 1961. It is through the MCP that the citizens of Malawi are mobilized to participate in the government. The MCP has both a women's league and a youth wing called the Malawi Young Pioneers. When special national tasks need to be done, it is the Young Pioneers who are most often called on to complete them. The MCP as a whole acts as a unifying force in the country.

Dr. Banda, the leader of the Malawi Congress party, is the life president of Malawi. He has the power to make decisions about every aspect of government. He is helped in ruling the country by the Malawian Parliament, which is modeled on the British Parliament. Of the seventy-five members of Parliament, sixty are elected and fifteen are appointed. The members are responsible for keeping the country running smoothly and for acting as intermediaries between the president and his people.

Malawi has a system of district councils. Both elected officials and traditional chiefs are represented on these councils. The councils bring government to the local areas, and they are responsible for providing their people with basic public services such as water supplies, roads, health centers, markets, and education.

Malawi has tried to be very practical in its foreign policies. The president believes that Malawi should be friendly to any country that can help it, regardless of the internal situation in that country. This policy has led Malawi into some difficult situations. The situation that causes the most problems is Malawi's relationship with South Africa. Malawi is economically dependent on South Africa and believes it must maintain a very open and friendly relationship. South Africa's apartheid policy has been widely condemned throughout the world and many African leaders have criticized Malawi for being friendly to such a nation. President Banda often has spoken out against the apartheid policy, but leaders in the other Southern African nations are angry because Malawi seems to them to be favoring South Africa and not supporting them in their efforts to help bring justice and freedom to South Africa.

## TOWNS AND CITIES

Another feature of modern Malawi that makes it different from the earlier Amaravi Confederation, or Akafula society, is its cities and towns. Although only about 10 percent of Malawians live in

*The building of the Southern Bottlers Union displays a black rooster, the symbol of the Malawi Congress party.*

these urban areas, they are a very important part of Malawi because the industry, commerce, government, and communication systems of the country center around them. Each major town in Malawi has its own distinctive history and atmosphere.

## BLANTYRE: CITY OF COMMERCE AND INDUSTRY

The southern region's city of Blantyre is the oldest and largest city in Malawi. Blantyre began as a small settlement that developed near the Church of Scotland's Blantyre Mission in the Shire Highlands. When the African Lakes Corporation put its headquarters there in 1880, the settlement began to grow. In 1882 the African Lakes Corporation built a house for the manager of the company. This house still stands and it is now the oldest house standing in Malawi. The settlement became a town in 1895, taking its name from the mission.

*Headquarters of the Bible Society of Malawi in Blantyre*

In 1907, another town began to grow up only five miles (eight kilometers) away where the railway line from Southern Rhodesia ended. This rapidly expanding town was named Limbe, and it became the headquarters of the prosperous Imperial Tobacco Company. In 1948, both Blantyre and Limbe became mayoralties, and were allowed to elect their own mayors and city councils. In 1965, the two towns were combined as the city of Blantyre-Limbe. In 1966, the twin cities became the city of Blantyre.

Today, the city still has two distinct centers linked by the five-mile (eight-kilometer) Kamuzu Highway. Halfway between the two centers, straddling the highway, is the Independence Arch—a white concrete arch that celebrates Malawi's freedom from colonial rule. Malawi's black, red, and green flag always flies here. Surrounded by hills with names like Ndirande, Michiru, Mpingwe, Bangwe, and Soche, Blantyre is the industrial, commercial, and communications center of the country. It has a major airport and a major railway depot. It is directly linked by road to every major town in Malawi.

*Waiting for public transportation in Blantyre*

*Offices of the British High Commission (left) and the building that houses the National Library Service (right) in Lilongwe*

## LILONGWE: AGRICULTURAL AND ADMINISTRATIVE CAPITAL

Lilongwe is the second-largest and fastest growing of Malawi's cities. Its name is taken from the river that runs through the center of town. It began as a small settlement that grew up around the colonial administrative center (the Boma), which was set up in 1902. For many years the most distinctive feature of Lilongwe was that it lay at the center of one of the largest farming areas in Malawi. In 1975, the capital was transferred to Lilongwe. Since then, the town has grown very fast.

The new capital city lies about three miles (five kilometers)

*Sugarcane on sale in a Lilongwe market (left)*
*and the control board (right) of a power station in the city*

from the old center of town. It is a planned city with lovely white
stone buildings and many parks. Most government departments,
ministries, and foreign embassies have moved to Lilongwe,
though the move has taken time and is not yet fully complete.
Parliament, for example, still meets in the old capital. The capital
of Malawi was moved to Lilongwe partly because it is in the
middle of the country. It was hoped that placing the capital here
with its new communication networks and new airport, would
help to shift some of the industrial and commercial wealth of the
south into the central region. Other attempts at development in
Lilongwe include the Lilongwe Land Development Scheme,
through which the government hopes to improve agricultural
production in this fertile area.

*Fruits and vegetables for sale in a Zomba market*

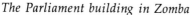

Lilongwe

Zomba

Blantyre

*The Parliament building in Zomba*

## ZOMBA: CITY OF HISTORY AND EDUCATION

The capital of Malawi used to be Zomba. Zomba, now the country's third-largest city, is situated at the foot of the Zomba Plateau. It was made the first capital of Malawi by the British colonial administration in 1891. The British established their capital there because it had a cool, wet climate that reminded them of their homeland. It was situated at the point where a number of slave routes met and the British hoped that their presence there would help end the slave trade in Malawi.

There are many old buildings in this quiet town. The Government Hostel was built in 1886 as a residence for Sir Harry Johnston, the first British commissioner of Nyasaland. The State House, with its lovely gardens, is very old. It is now the official residence of the president of Malawi. Zomba is the site of the King's African Rifles Monument, which is a brick monument built in memory of all those Malawians who died in World War I while serving in the KAR. Since the capital was moved to Lilongwe, Zomba has become a university town. Chancellor College, the central section of the University of Malawi, is located in Zomba.

*Kamuzu Academy in Mtunthama*

## EDUCATION

Since independence, many new schools have been built. The demand for education is very high, but Malawi faces a number of problems. It is expensive to build and equip new schools and it takes time to train all the teachers needed.

After completing eight years of primary education and taking a national examination, a student receives a school-leaving certificate. The best students from primary schools go on to secondary school, where they complete two years of course work and an examination. If they pass the examination they are awarded a junior certificate and may go on to a technical training program or a vocational school. The best students will continue in secondary school to complete the requirements for the Malawi certificate of education. This takes another two years. Only after completing this rigorous course can Malawians apply to the University of Malawi for higher education.

The University of Malawi has a number of different colleges. Bunda College is located in the central region near Lilongwe and is an agricultural college. The Polytechnic in Blantyre trains Malawians to be engineers, accountants, business managers, or other technical personnel. Chancellor College is a combination of the old teacher-training college, the Institute of Public Administration (where civil servants and lawyers were trained), and the Liberal Arts College. The Kamuzu School of Nursing, another college within the University of Malawi, is in Lilongwe.

## HEALTH

Health has been a special priority of the president. The major hospitals in Blantyre and Zomba have been expanded and new hospitals have been built. Clinics and health extension services have been set up all over the country. As with education, Malawi faces shortages of money and trained people in its attempt to provide good health care to all its people.

One area in which Malawi has seen some great successes is in its campaign to eliminate infectious diseases and epidemics. The World Health Organization has helped the country in its efforts to fight smallpox, malaria, and tuberculosis by free vaccination and treatment programs. The British Leprosy Relief Association has worked with the government to eliminate leprosy and it has been remarkably successful, especially in southern Malawi. Another area that has been important in Malawi's efforts to fight disease is health education. Malawi has a number of programs teaching cleanliness, sanitation, and basic health care. Education about nutrition and programs that help provide fresh fruits and vegetables to all rural areas are important.

# Chapter 6

# PEOPLE AND
##  THEIR LIFE-STYLES

Over seven million people live in Malawi, making it one of the most densely populated areas in Africa. The highest concentrations of people are found in the rich agricultural districts north of Blantyre, around the southern tea-growing areas, and on the Lilongwe plain.

The population of Malawi is growing very fast. From 1921 to 1960 the population doubled, and it is still increasing. With Malawi's high population density, the rapid increase in the numbers of people to be supported has put strains on Malawi's ability to feed its people. In addition, industry and commerce have not developed fast enough to provide jobs for all the people who need them. This leads to unemployment and even more pressure on the land. The problem has been made worse by the high levels of immigration into Malawi from the surrounding countries.

There are three main racial groups in Malawi: African, European, and Asian. The Asians come mostly from Pakistan, India, and Sri Lanka, and they comprise about 5 percent of

Malawi's total population. The Asians live mostly in the urban areas of the southern region, where they occupy positions in trade and business. The Europeans, who are mostly of British origin, are concentrated in the southern region. Most of the Europeans in Malawi are concerned with business or farming. Some Europeans have come into the country temporarily as diplomats (ambassadors or embassy staff) or as technical advisers and managers for projects that are set up by foreign aid agencies. There are a number of European missionaries in Malawi.

The African people of Malawi are quite diverse. The largest ethnic groups are the Chewa, who dominate the southern and central regions; and the Ngoni, who live mostly in the central and northern regions, especially along the lakeshore. Other significant groups include the Yao and the Lomwe, who live mostly in the southern part of the country; and the Tumbuka who live in the northern region along with the Tonga and the Nkhonde. Although the African population in Malawi is diverse and there are differences between the groups, they are generally closely related. There is very little of the tension between ethnic groups that one finds in some other African countries. For the most part, the people identify themselves as Malawians, and they choose to emphasize their unity rather than their differences.

There are almost twice as many women as men living in Malawi. The most important reason for this is that almost a quarter of the adult male population of Malawi lives and works in other African countries because jobs are not easy to find in their own country and land resources are becoming more and more scarce. Most of the men who leave Malawi go to work in the mines of Zambia, Zimbabwe, and South Africa, where they are known for their diligence and hard work. Some migrate

*To earn a living, many Malawi men go to South Africa to work in the gold mines.*

individually, often following in the footsteps of their president and walking hundreds of miles south to find employment. The men used to be absent for about two years, after which time they returned to Malawi. Once their savings were used up again, they tended to go back to their jobs in faraway countries. Today, because of the intervention of Malawi's president, migrants stay a much shorter period in South Africa before returning to Malawi. Dr. Banda insisted on the shorter absences as a way of making the system less destructive to Malawian family life. Many migrants still return time and again to their foreign jobs.

The effects of this migrant labor system are serious. In some areas, especially in the northern part of the country, there are not enough able-bodied men to effectively cultivate the fields. This makes it difficult for the people who are left to grow enough food for themselves, and the earnings that the migrants send back to their families are often not enough to support them. In addition,

*A typical rural village in the Angoni Highlands*

the system of migrant labor breaks up families and makes marriages very unstable. Since the family unit is the center of Malawian society, this tears the fabric of Malawian communities and produces very serious social consequences. Nevertheless, the system is likely to continue unless Malawi can find a way to provide good employment opportunities to those people who now migrate to find work.

## LIVING

Most people in Malawi (more than 90 percent) live in traditional agricultural villages. These villages are generally small since the larger a village grows, the longer the distance between the houses and the fields that are worked by the villagers. The villages are often linked to one another, to their associated fields, and to the nearest water source by well-worn footpaths. Villages usually consist of homes surrounding a cleared area where grain is dried and pounded into flour. Behind the dwellings there often might be a grain-storage bin made out of woven bamboo and standing on stilts to keep out mice. A woven bamboo pigeon house and an enclosure for chickens might stand in this area. The dwellings that make up the traditional villages are small round thatch houses. They are constructed with a frame made of wood poles that are covered with mud, which hardens as it dries. The thatch roof is made of dried grass and replaced every so often when it becomes too tattered or waterlogged. These houses, because they are made of dried mud, are usually very cool in the hot season. They always are kept clean and neat.

Today, the traditional village dwellings are more often being replaced by newer buildings that show a European influence.

Houses are more often rectangular now, built of handmade bricks and roofed with corrugated aluminum. The newer houses are generally larger and set farther apart than the more traditional dwellings. In some cases the house will have a small "driveway" bordered with flowers and a garden fence. In urban areas the European influence is stronger. People live in Western-style houses that are often provided by the government. Around the edges of Malawi's cities, many live in slum areas. Here there are few real houses and people live in temporary shelters that they have constructed out of scrap materials. Clean water is scarce in these areas and sanitation is poor. Disease is a problem. The Malawian government is trying to provide the people who live in these areas with housing, but it does not have enough money to cope with the number of people who come into the urban areas every year.

## THE EXTENDED FAMILY

The family is the most important social unit in Malawian society. It is the family group that works together in the fields and it is often one family that makes up a village. The Malawian concept of family is not the same as the Western idea of family. A Malawian family does not just include immediate relatives— mother, father, sisters, and brothers—but a wide range of relatives. Each member of the immediate family might be responsible for other relatives in a variety of ways. For example a man is responsible by custom for the well-being and education of his sisters' children, and they call him their father. His sons and daughters (whom a Westerner would call cousins) will be their sisters and brothers. Families often are close-knit and it is believed

*A boatman and his children on the shores of Lake Malawi*

that everything should be shared, both good and bad fortune. Thus, if one family member is wealthy, he or she is expected to share that wealth with the other members of the extended family. If one member is in trouble, he or she can go to any member of the family and ask for help. This concept of the extended family acts as a kind of social insurance system. Today, especially in the urban areas, the extended family is breaking down more and more.

It is not only the concept of what a family consists of that is different in Malawi. Family structure is different from the traditional family structure in most Western countries. Family property in Malawi, for example, is passed down from father to his sister's son rather than from father to son. In many Western countries the wife becomes part of her husband's family when she marries. This is signified by the wife taking the husband's name. But when a couple marries in Malawi, the husband is considered a

*The traditional dress of Malawi women includes cloths that can be wrapped around the body to create a pouch for carrying a baby.*

part of his wife's family. The man leaves his own village when he marries, builds a house in his wife's village, and farms land for his wife's family. The couple's children are considered to be a part of the wife's family. This system of matriarchy gives social power to women in Malawi with the result that they are often less oppressed than women in traditional Western marriages.

## DRESS

The traditional dress for women in Malawi consists of a series of cloths that are wrapped around the body in different ways. The cloths are usually very colorful and a woman might wear two or three as a dress and another for her head. Cloths can be tied in a way that creates a pouch in which the woman can carry a baby. Babies are carried everywhere on their mother's or sister's back in this way.

*Fish is an important source of protein for Malawians; here it is being smoked on wooden racks.*

Traditional dress for men differs from ethnic group to ethnic group. The Yao men, for example, have mostly adopted the dress of their Arab trading partners, and they wear white tunics over white trousers. Many Malawians today have adopted European-style dress. Out of respect for custom, it is still against the law for women to wear trousers, shorts, or short skirts, as it is considered offensive for a woman to show any part of her leg above the knee. Although these laws might seem to be incredibly restrictive to Westerners, the majority of Malawians strongly support the dress code.

## FOOD

The most common food in Malawi is *nsima,* a kind of thick porridge made of ground maize (corn). The nsima is usually eaten with some kind of sauce called *ndiwo.* The ndiwo is often quite spicy and usually consists of boiled leaves or meat with other vegetables such as carrots, tomatoes, and potatoes when they are available. Other common foods include sweet potatoes, pumpkins, and a root crop similar to a potato called cassava. Traditionally the men and women in a village would eat separately. The men would eat first, and the women and children would eat later. This custom is not as common now. Today in the cities many Malawians eat some Western food, but nsima and ndiwo is still offered in almost every household. Sometimes rice is offered as a substitute, but most Malawians prefer nsima.

## RELIGION

Many Malawians hold traditional religious beliefs. They believe in a supreme being called *Mulungu*, which is usually translated as "God." They believe in ancestral spirits who can affect the lives of the living. This is, in some ways, the extension of the concept of family. Even family members who have died are honored and respected. There are spirits associated with natural phenomena like wind, rain, or the sun. Belief in these spirits is strong in the rural areas, but it is slowly eroding in the urban areas.

Apart from the traditional religions, Christianity and Islam have become established in Malawi. Most Christians belong to one of four major churches: Presbyterian, Catholic, Seventh-Day Adventist, and Anglican. Of the four main denominations, the Church of Central Africa Presbyterian (CCAP) is the largest. Over 20 percent of Malawians belong to the Roman Catholic church. The Anglican and Seventh-Day Adventist are both smaller, with less than 10 percent of the population belonging to them. There are a number of very small churches. Some of these are the result of missionary activity, but many are entirely Malawian in their origin and are varied in their beliefs and practices. Islam was originally brought to Malawi by Arab traders and at first most Muslims in Malawi were from the Yao tribe. Recently the Muslim community has been experiencing a religious revival encouraged by funds from oil-rich Arab states. Many new mosques, the Muslim house of worship, have been built all over the country, and many new schools have been built.

## LANGUAGE

The official languages of Malawi are Chichewa (the language of the largest ethnic group) and English. Most people in the cities and towns are fluent in English, but in the rural areas Chichewa is the most common language spoken and over 75 percent of the people understand it. Other local languages are spoken too, such as Yao, Tumbuka, Ngoni, and Lomwe. Among the migrant workers a new language has developed, influenced by their life in the mining compounds of South Africa and Zimbabwe. This language is called Chilapalapa, and it is a mixture of the local Malawian languages, English, and Afrikaans (the language of the white Afrikaners of South Africa), and the Bantu languages of South Africa like Zulu and Xhosa. Chilapalapa is almost entirely a spoken language. It has no dictionaries or grammar books.

## WORKING

The majority of Malawians are self-employed in growing food for their own use. The agricultural year in Malawi usually begins when the rains arrive in late October or November. The ground is then broken up using the traditional hoe. The crops are planted, usually maize and pumpkins or gourds, and the fields are then left alone until they have to be weeded, usually two or three times before the harvest. The weeding is mostly done by hand, although hoes are sometimes used. This time of year (around March) is called "the time of hunger," because the new grain is not ready but the stores of last year's harvest are being used up. It is the time of disease because there are not many green vegetables to be found.

At the end of March, the pumpkins and other vegetables begin to ripen. The maize ripens in May and then has to be harvested. The maize is harvested by hand. Once harvested, it is dried and then pounded into flour for nsima. This is the busiest time of year. Throughout the growing season the crops need to be protected from wild animals, especially baboons and wild pigs who can devastate a field very quickly. Platforms on stilts surround the fields and watchers are there all day and all night to scare off the animals. Animals are scared away by making loud noises or setting fake traps.

Traditionally Malawians had a clear-cut division of labor; everyone had his or her own chores to do. This is still true for many rural Malawians. Generally, the men are responsible for keeping the house in good shape and for thatching its roof. Men are responsible for making fences and mortars where the grain is pounded, and for sewing, spinning, and weaving. It is the men who carve wood and work with iron. In lakeshore communities, the men do most of the fishing and they make the fishing canoes. In Malawi, it is the women who do most of the agricultural work. The men will help with the heavy fieldwork if they are there, but this is most often done by women. Women brew beer, cut wood,

*The men make the canoes that they use for fishing, and the fish are transported in hand-woven baskets.*

collect water, gather the harvest, pound the grain, look after the children, and do the cooking. The burden on women is greater in families where the men have gone to work in foreign countries because the women then have to do the men's jobs as well as their own. This is one of the many problems created by the migrant labor system.

## CEREMONIES AND CELEBRATIONS

Malawians do not just work. They often take time to celebrate life and have fun. The two most important and joyous occasions for Malawians are the passage from childhood to adulthood and weddings.

The passage from childhood to adulthood is marked by various ceremonies. The boys, and often the girls, who are about to become adults in the Malawian community, are taken separately to "camps" in the bush where they stay for as long as two months. At these camps they are trained to act as adults. They are taught about the history and traditions of their people. The girls are taught to be good wives and mothers. When the training period is over, the children are given new names, and it is then an insult to call them by their childhood names. The boys move out of their mothers' houses and live either alone or with other boys. Once the ceremonies and celebrations are over, the children are then considered adults and they are given the responsibilities and privileges of an adult in the community.

The traditional Malawian marriage ceremonies involve the whole village. The bridegroom begins by asking his uncle or another important member of his family to act in his behalf in negotiating the wedding contract with the bride's family. If these negotiations are successfully completed, then the couple are considered to be engaged. Gifts are often exchanged at this point, and the couple will visit and get to know each other's families. In some parts of Malawi the man will be asked to compensate the bride's family for the loss of one of their members. This is called bridewealth. In other parts of the country, the man may be asked to build a house for himself and his bride in her village. When both families agree that it is time for the wedding to take place, a wedding feast will be held. Often there will be dancing throughout the day and night. The whole village will witness the marriage and they become responsible for helping to make the marriage a success. Near the end of the ceremony the couple is given marriage instruction by the village elders.

Today, in the urban areas, the process of marriage is often very complicated with European and traditional customs getting mixed together. A wedding ceremony is held in a church or government office. This is followed by a reception in town and often a second feast, or a traditional ceremony, in the village. Sometimes, if the bride and the groom are from different areas of the country, two separate village feasts must be added to the Western-style wedding in town.

## PASTIMES

*Chiwewe* is a form of jump rope played by children in Malawi. One player squats on the ground and swings a weighted rope around his or her head. The other players, who stand in a circle around the rope swinger, have to jump over the rope. The person who does not clear the rope has to become the next swinger. *Mpira* is another game played by children in Malawi. It is a ball game. The players stand in a circle and throw the ball to each other in a certain rhythm. Any player who drops the ball or throws it to the wrong person in the wrong order or in the wrong rhythm, drops out of the game. This is a very hard game for non-Malawians to learn.

When not playing games like chiwewe and mpira, Malawian children often play with homemade toys. One common toy, seen especially in the cities and towns, is a tire that is driven and guided by a stick. Another common toy is a car, jeep, or helicopter made from wire. These wire vehicles are very carefully constructed so that they can be steered using a wheel attached to a long stick. Tourists to Malawi are often fascinated by the intricate wire toys that the children make.

# Chapter 7

# CULTURE—TRADITIONAL AND MODERN

Modern Malawi really has two cultures that exist side by side and influence each other. One culture is older and developed before any Europeans or Westerners came to the area. The other culture has developed more recently in response to the demands and situations of everyday life in modern Malawi. The two cultures are not always distinct from one another. Elements from one culture may be borrowed for the other. Nevertheless, it is important to recognize the changes that have taken place in Malawian culture as the country has developed.

## LITERATURE

In the past all of Malawi's literature was spoken rather than written. This rich heritage of oral literature included traditional tales, songs, riddles, and proverbs.

Traditional songs are usually sung for a purpose. There are songs that are associated with different kinds of work and songs that are sung only with certain dances or at a certain kind of festival. Some songs are used to make comments, either good or bad, about society and the events and people of the time. A singer of such songs might praise a local hero or criticize someone who has committed a crime. At certain times, the singer would even be allowed to criticize and mock the chief or leader of the community for not doing a good job. This is one way in which Malawians kept their chiefs from becoming too powerful.

Malawian proverbs and traditional tales have a purpose in the society. Proverbs and tales are told to children (and sometimes adults) to teach them about history, morals, religion, social customs, and how to handle relationships with other people in the community.

Written literature in Malawi began in 1934 when Samuel Yosia Ntara published a work with the title, *Man in Africa*. Since then, a solid literary tradition has been built by such writers as Audrey Kachingwe, David Rubadiri, and Willy Zingani. One of the greatest of Malawi's writers is Legson Kayira. Although Kayira is a Malawian, he has lived most of his life outside Malawi. When he was young, he walked over 2,000 miles (3,219 kilometers) to the Sudan in North Africa carrying only a Bible and a copy of *Pilgrim's Progress*. He has never returned to live in his homeland. His first book was an autobiography called *I Will Try*, and it won an award when it was published in 1965. Later, Kayira wrote three novels in English and other stories in Chichewa.

Creative writing in both English and Chichewa is encouraged in Malawi. In the early 1970s, the Writers' Group of Malawi began to publish a journal called *Odi*, which accepted contributions from anyone whose work met certain standards. It is hoped that this will encourage new writers to publish their work.

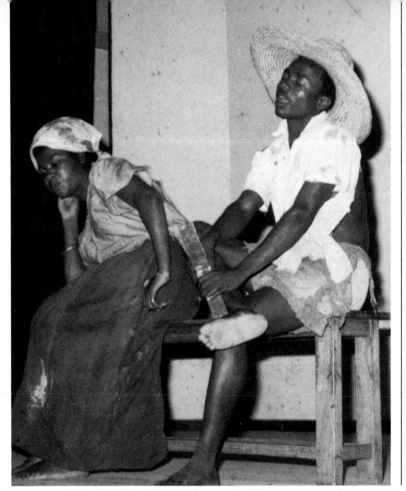

*A locally written play being performed at the National Schools Drama Festival*

The Malawi Broadcasting Corporation has encouraged the development of drama and poetry by broadcasting locally written plays and poetry readings. The National Schools Drama Festival, established soon after independence, encourages drama by holding a nationwide drama competition. A number of independent theater companies produce a variety of locally written and often improvised plays.

Although a literary tradition is being encouraged, the traditional oral literature has not disappeared. There have been a number of attempts to preserve this rich and varied heritage. Many of the old proverbs, tales, and riddles are being written down and many of the old songs are still taught to the children so that they will not be forgotten.

*A craft house at the Mua Craft Center*

## ARTS AND CRAFTS

The earliest form of painting in Malawi was the rock painting that appears on rock faces, in rock shelters, and in shallow caves all over the country, but particularly in the northern and the central regions. These rock paintings include both stylistic drawings of animals and trees and geometric patterns in red and white. They are thought to have been painted by the hunting and gathering groups that lived in the area before the Bantu migration.

Wood carving began fairly early in Malawi's history. One of the first type of wood carving was the masks that were carved to be used in the various rituals in Malawian life. Later such items as pipe stems, bowls, and knife scabbards were carved. After the Europeans arrived in the area, the Malawians turned their skill to carving objects for sale and today tourists in Malawi can still buy

*Tourists examining woven mats and baskets in a market*

beautiful carvings. Many of the carvings are made of ebony, a very dark wood that is quite rare.

Like wood carving, traditional skills such as basket and mat weaving and pottery were originally developed for practical reasons rather than as art. Today these crafts produce items for sale to tourists as well as the practical items they have produced for generations.

The importance of practical training in Malawi has meant that art education often has been a low priority. Nevertheless, informal and formal art groups have sprung up, and evening classes in Western art techniques are offered at the university. A number of Malawian artists have sold their work, often to tourists, but no one artist has developed a large following within the country. Modern paintings usually deal with the colorful scenes of everyday life in Malawi.

# MUSIC AND DANCE

There are a variety of traditional musical instruments in Malawi. The *chimwenyumwenyu* is one example, a kind of fiddle played with one string attached to a hollow gourd. The *limba*, another instrument, has six strings and its gourd has metal, seed, or shell rattles attached to it. The *timibila*, or *magologodo*, is a kind of Malawian piano with metal keys. It is much smaller than a Western piano and it is usually carried in the hands and played with the thumbs. The *lipenga*, or *nkhombo*, is a kind of horn made out of a gourd, while the *chakwana* is something like a flute. It is usually made out of bamboo. There is a traditional xylophone made out of wooden slats of differing lengths and thicknesses that have been placed on two banana stalks.

Many other instruments exist in Malawi. The most common musical instrument is the drum. There are many different kinds of drums in Malawi. The smallest is the *kandimbe*, which is only 4 or 5 inches (102 or 127 millimeters) across. The largest drum is the *mpanje*. The mpanje can be more than 5 feet (1.5 meters) long. Some drums, like the *mpangula*, are beaten by hand while others, like the *mfinta*, are beaten using sticks. The *nthiki* and *mvema* drums are barrel shaped, but the *kamanga* is shaped like a wine glass. The *murumbo* is round and shallow like a bowl, while the *khunto* is shaped like a narrow cylinder. All these drums might be played together at one time in a kind of drum orchestra, but they can be played separately. Malawian drum players have to be very skilled, and many spend most of their lives being trained by those drummers who have become very good and are considered masters.

Music, in Malawi, is rarely played alone. It is usually

accompanied by dancing. Malawi has a wide variety of traditional dances celebrating various aspects of life. Such dances include the Ngoni war dance known as *ingoma*, and the *gule wa mkulu*, a Chewa dance that is performed during the ceremonies marking the passage between childhood and adulthood. During the ingoma dances, the dancers wear shawls and kilts made of the skin of leopards and other wildcats. They have high headdresses made from black feathers, and they carry spears and large shields made out of cow skin. They accompany their dances with foot stamping and beautiful songs. The gule wa mkulu was originally practiced in secret and younger people were not allowed to see it. The dancers wear very elaborate costumes, which completely hide them so that the spectators cannot see who they are. Some wear frightening or amusing masks and cover their bodies in mud or ash. Others wear costumes made of bamboo and banana leaves. These costumes make them look like animals such as an elephant or an antelope. Traditionally the dancers were thought to become possessed by the spirit of the animals they represented. The gule wa mkulu dance is very energetic and it is accompanied by drums and hand clapping.

Another traditional dance is the *vimbuza*, or *masawe*, which is danced to help exorcise evil spirits. The *malipenga* dance, performed mostly by men, and the *chiwoda*, which is performed by women, were developed only in the early twentieth century. The malipenga was modeled after the movements of Western military marching bands and it began among the members of the King's African Rifles in World War I. Other dances include the hunter's dance of the *Tumbuka*, which is called *urumba*, and the mourning dance, which is called the *nkwenda*.

Many of the traditional dances of Malawi are still performed.

*Malawians have no problems mixing modern and traditional cultures. A member of Parliament has put a skirt on over his suit (above) and joined in a traditional dance.*

They can be seen at national celebrations where dance troupes from all over the country gather. Some of the dances, such as the ingoma, are now danced almost only for entertainment. Some, like the gule wa mkulu and the vimbuza, are still danced in their traditional contexts and they still play an important role in the society.

In urban areas more Westernized forms of dance such as disco and reggae have become popular. Local musicians play in nightclubs and hotels. The most popular kinds of music in the cities are reggae, jazz, and disco. Some African musicians are now combining Western styles with traditional African styles, and performing a distinctive music of their own. Although electric guitars, pianos, and other Western instruments are used, traditional instruments might be played alongside them.

Although new cultural influences in literature, art, and music can be seen in modern Malawi, and especially in the cities, it is clear that the older traditional culture is still strong.

# Chapter 8

# A NATION OF FARMERS

Since independence, one of the government's most important tasks has been to keep Malawi peaceful and prosperous. One of the things that this involves is feeding Malawi's people. Unlike many countries in Africa, Malawi has not concentrated on rapid industrialization to make the country prosperous. Instead, realizing that the country's greatest resources are its fertile land and hardworking people, Dr. Banda's government has put most of its time and energy into developing the agricultural sector of the economy.

## AGRICULTURE

More than 10 percent of Malawi's land is under cultivation. There are two types of crops grown in Malawi: subsistence crops, which are those grown for food at the local level; and cash crops, which are grown on a large scale and sold to national or international buyers. Beans, millet, and vegetables are examples of crops grown for food. Cassava is important as a food crop and it is grown all over the country.

*Cassava, a rootstock, (young plants shown at left) is grown throughout Malawi. Maize (top left) is the most important subsistence crop and tobacco (above) is a cash crop.*

The most important subsistence crop is maize, or corn. Maize is the staple food crop in Malawi. Although it is the most important subsistence crop in Malawi, maize is grown also as a cash crop. The plains around Lilongwe are ideal for maize growing and the yields are very high. Maize production has been increasing over the last ten years.

Tobacco is another cash crop. Most Malawian tobacco is flue-cured, like the tobacco grown in Virginia in the United States. This means that it is dried by heated air that seals in the rich

*Some tobacco is dried in the sun (left) and some of it is steamed (right).*

perfume and color of the leaves. Flue-cured tobacco is used in cigarettes. Some Malawian tobacco is dried in the sun or by fire. Fire-dried tobacco is used for pipes and it often takes on the aroma of the wood that is burned to dry it.

Tea is Malawi's most important export crop. The first tea in Malawi was planted at Blantyre Mission in 1878, making Malawi the first African country to grow tea. This crop grows best in the highlands of the southern region around Mount Mulanje and the Thoylo Mountains. It is grown on large plantations usually owned by foreign companies. The tea is picked by hand. The tea pickers are given huge baskets to put the tea in. They pluck only the top three leaves from each stalk. It is a slow process and many people are needed to pick tea in each field at harvest time.

Coffee was the first cash crop grown in Malawi. In the early twentieth century, disease destroyed most of the plants. Recently, because of the development of new types of coffee plants and better methods of cultivation, coffee has again become an important cash crop.

*Tea pickers use huge baskets to collect the tea.*

*Barges filled with sugar travel on the Shire River.*

Cotton is another cash crop grown mostly in the lower areas of the country, especially in the hot, dry Rift valley where the Shire River meanders. One of the most important cotton plantations is the Chikwawa Cotton Development Scheme, which began in 1968 and has been productive since then. Sugarcane is grown in the Rift valley. The Sucoma Sugar Estates, which lie quite near Chikwawa, provide employment for many people in the area, and the money that the government gets from selling sugar is vital to Malawi's economy. Another experimental sugar plantation was recently started at Dwangwa in the northern region.

Groundnuts are grown mostly in the central region around Lilongwe and Kasungu. They are used both for food and to make oil for cooking. Macadamia nuts, grown mostly in the southern region, have recently become popular. Tung nuts, which are not eaten but are used to make the oil that goes into oil-based paints, are important in earning money for the country.

*A forest on Zomba Plateau (left) and a Zebu bull (right)*

Food crops are not the only plants that are grown and cultivated in Malawi. Malawi has an important forestry program. The wood planted in the forestry replantation schemes is mostly softwood. It is grown for pulpwood, which is used for making paper. Some wood is used for fuel or for building and construction. There are two main forestry schemes. One is the Viphya Pulpwood Scheme in the country's northern region. The other, which is somewhat smaller, is on Zomba Plateau. A new scheme, with a pulp mill at Chinteche on the northern lakeshore, will help the forestry industry to expand once it is completed.

Cattle are the most important livestock in Malawi. There are two main breeds. The Zebu cattle have a hump that looks like the hump of a camel and the Ngoni cattle are distinguished by their long curved horns. Cattle are kept for beef and milk and they are important in the culture. A large herd of cattle is a sign of great wealth in Malawi. The larger the cattle herd, the wealthier its owner. Most cattle in Malawi do not have a high milk yield. Recently Malawi has imported some high milk-yield dairy cows so that it will be able to provide milk to everyone. These cows are very expensive and are usually only owned by large estates. They are not very hardy and are difficult to raise. Until a new breed is found that is resistant to disease, high milk-yield cows will be rare in Malawi.

Fish play two important roles in Malawi's economy. Fish provide a source of protein in the diet of Malawians, and they are exported both as food and for aquariums. Lake Malawi has nearly 270 types of fish. Two hundred forty of those types are found only in Malawi. Some of these fish are edible, the most delicious being a fish known as chambo. Others are not known for how they taste, but rather for their brilliantly colored beauty. It is these fish that are sold to aquarium owners all over the world.

## NATURAL RESOURCES

Apart from the land and its people, Malawi's largest and most valuable natural resource is its waterways. The lakes and rivers of Malawi provide an easy and relatively cheap way of transporting people and goods throughout much of the country. They also provide electricity. Malawi has a very high hydroelectric potential. The most valuable hydroelectric resources are centered on the rapids and waterfalls of the middle Shire River. So far, two hydroelectric power plants have been constructed. The biggest is at Nkula Falls, and the other is at Tedzani Falls. Harnessing the power of the Shire's fast running water to generate electricity saves Malawi much money that might otherwise have to be used to buy electricity or fuel from other nations.

Malawi does not have the same kind of mineral wealth that most of its neighbors in Southern Africa have. That is one of the main reasons for the lower level of industrial development in Malawi, and the emphasis on agricultural development. Malawi does have four coalfields, two in the north and two in the south. These fields have not been exploited until very recently. The coal is very difficult to get out and it has not been valuable enough to justify the expense of extracting it. Other mineral deposits in Malawi include bauxite, phosphate, and titanium. Like the coal, these deposits are in small, isolated areas, and they are too expensive to mine and process.

## INDUSTRY

Although Malawi is mostly an agricultural country and the government has concentrated its resources in developing that sector of the economy, the country has witnessed a remakable development of its industry. The growth of industry in Malawi can be largely attributed to the activities of the Malawi Development Corporation (MDC), which was formed in 1964. The MDC has encouraged the formation of many companies. It supports the policy of Malawi's government to reduce the country's dependence on foreign imported goods by producing some things locally. The development of local industry was made possible by the cheap power provided by the two hydroelectric plants at Tedzani and Nkula Falls. The fastest-growing sector in industry is manufacturing.

Over half of the manufacturing companies in Malawi have their headquarters in Blantyre. There are two main reasons for this. First, the city provides the largest market in Malawi for manufactured goods. Second, Blantyre has strong communication, transportation, and trade links with the rest of the country, and with the world.

The largest manufacturing industry in Malawi is agricultural processing. This is not surprising since the most important local natural resource is the land and its produce. Tea, tobacco, groundnuts, rice, sugar, and cotton all require processing before they can be sold. Malawi has taken over the processing of most of these crops from the foreign-owned companies that originally did the processing. In addition, the country has begun to develop a canning industry so that its agricultural produce can be preserved and sold cheaply to people in the remote areas of Malawi and in the neighboring countries.

Other manufacturing industries include cement production, furniture construction, vehicle repairs, distilling alcohol, paint production, soap and detergent production, clothing and shoe production, printing, publishing, and cigarette manufacture. All these industries are small, local industries that can be developed at a relatively low cost using local materials. The goods that are produced are sold at a lower price than the similar goods that are imported. This means that those goods are then available to more Malawians and the money paid for them stays inside the country instead of being paid to foreigners.

Although it is the most important, manufacturing is not the only form of industry in Malawi. The traditional craft industries of Malawi are being developed also. It has been estimated that almost 90 percent of Malawians are skilled in a traditional craft. This is a valuable resource that should not be wasted. Craft production is usually small scale and based on local demand. Specialties of Malawian crafts include beautiful baskets, patterned

*Malawi has many spectacular vistas, such as this view across the Zomba Plateau.*

woven grass carpets, the making of spears, shields, and knives, and carvings made out of ebony, ivory, and malachite, a dark green semiprecious stone.

With its beautiful and varied scenery, its many national parks, and its spectacular lake, Malawi's tourist industry is an important part of the economy that has grown fairly fast. Tourists do come from all over the world to visit the country, but most of the visitors are from other parts of Southern Africa. This is mostly because airfares from Europe and the United States are very high, while it is quite cheap to travel between countries within Southern Africa.

The building and construction industry is growing fast, especially as more and more people move into the towns and cities. The Malawi Housing Corporation plans to build more than four hundred houses every year in Blantyre and Lilongwe to try and keep up with the need for housing. The transport industry, which is closely related to building and construction, is important. More and more roads and railways are needed to help transport food and manufactured goods to markets and to accommodate the growing numbers of tourists. The need for roads and railways, like the need for housing, generally is larger than the available resources.

## TRADE AND TRANSPORTATION

The most obvious characteristic of Malawi's trade is that it tends to export raw materials and import manufactured goods. Since raw materials are usually cheaper, this tendency leads to an imbalance in the country's trade.

Malawi's largest trading partner is Great Britain. South Africa, the United States, and The Netherlands export goods to Malawi and import Malawian products. Malawi is trying to increase its trade with the surrounding African countries as a cooperative venture that would benefit both Malawi and its African trading partners. Malawi is a member of the Southern African Development Coordination Conference (SADCC). SADCC includes nine member states who are trying to lessen their economic dependence on South Africa by trading with each other and utilizing each other's resources. Malawi's largest potential for trade is with Zambia and Zimbabwe, the country's closest and wealthiest neighbors. Mozambique could be an important trading

*The railway that connects Malawi and Mozambique*

partner with Malawi, since it has the ports and facilities Malawi needs to export its goods. Mozambique, however, is torn by a civil war, and Malawi is forced to export all its goods through South Africa.

Trade is impossible without some form of transportation for the goods to be traded. The most important form of transport in Malawi is water transport. In the past, Arab dhows and local fishing canoes, called *bwato*, were important in transporting people, ivory, and fish across the lake to be traded or sold. Today Lake Malawi has two main passenger boats that travel on the lake. These boats are named the *Ilala* and the *Chauncy Maples*. Malawi has a number of cargo boats. Many Malawians, however, still use the canoes and dhows that were used by their ancestors.

Malawi has a system of railways. The country is linked by rail to two east coast ports: Beira and Nacala. Both ports are in Mozambique and the railway lines are frequently impassable

*There are relatively few cars in Malawi, so many Malawians walk or travel by bus.*

because of the civil war there. The headquarters of Malawi Railways is in Limbe, Blantyre's twin city. The main railway lines run from Limbe to the lakeshore at Chipoka and Salima and then to Lilongwe; from Limbe to Nacala and from Limbe southward to Beira. There is also a railway line planned to go to Chipata, on the western border of the country.

The railways are not only used to export goods, they are used to transport goods within the country. Roads are used in this way too. Malawi's road system has developed rapidly. Roads link Malawi with all of the surrounding countries. There is one main two-lane highway that runs north to south. This is called the M1 and it is tarred for most of its length. There are roads that branch off the main highway, reaching every major town and most of the rural areas.

Malawi has two main airports. In 1967, the same year that Air Malawi became an independent airline, the Blantyre airport at Chileka was expanded to handle international flights. Recently, a new, larger, and more modern airport, named after the president, was opened near Lilongwe. Air transport is still very expensive in Malawi and most Malawians are unable to take advantage of its comforts.

Since air travel is so expensive and there are relatively few cars, most Malawians still travel by foot. Today, many people walk as much as ten miles (sixteen kilometers) to work every day. One modern invention that is relatively inexpensive and available to many Malawians is the bicycle, and in the city "rush hours" bicycles line either side of the main roads as people travel to and from their businesses. There is a good bus system, which covers most areas in Malawi. The buses are quite cheap and many Malawians use them.

# FUTURE PROSPECTS

In its attempt to modernize and raise the standard of living for its people, the government of Malawi has been very wise to utilize its greatest resources in the land and its hardworking people. The country's attempts at development have shown success in certain areas. Until recently, Malawi has, indeed, been able to feed its people and even export food crops to some of its neighbors. This is a great achievement. But Malawians face enormous problems in the future development of their country.

With no easily exploitable minerals, and little extra money to build the necessary factories, roads, railways, and communications systems, Malawi will find it difficult to industrialize fast enough to provide jobs for its rapidly growing population. Furthermore, if the pressure of people on the land increases, it is likely that agricultural productivity will decrease. This means that Malawi will find it increasingly difficult to feed its people. The problem is made worse by the fact that, in recent years, more than half a million refugees have fled into Malawi from Mozambique. These people need to be fed and housed. It is this problem, and the droughts of 1986 and 1987, that has forced Malawi to import basic foodstuffs in recent years.

As is true of most of Malawi's imports, the grain that was imported came from South Africa. Because it had to be transported by road, it was quite expensive and Malawi's national debt increased dramatically. Malawi's dependence on South Africa, both for imports and for export facilities as well as for jobs for many of its people, is another enormous problem facing the country. Until the civil war now raging in Mozambique ends, or a railway can be built through Zambia to the west coast, little can

be done to lessen Malawi's dependence on South Africa. Furthermore, even if such a railway were built and the country could export and import goods without using South African facilities, Malawi still would not have the resources to provide sufficient opportunities to keep people from migrating to the rich South African gold and diamond mines to work.

The problems seem enormous. Nevertheless, there is reason to hope in Malawi. The land is still fertile, and many effective schemes have been instituted to make it more productive. Unlike many of its neighbors in Africa, Malawi is a peaceful country where development can proceed without being disrupted by war and conflict. Malawi's people continue to strive for improvement and peace, and their indomitable spirit is Malawi's greatest hope.

## Map Key

| | |
|---|---|
| Balaka | D6 |
| Blantyre | E6 |
| Chilumba | D5 |
| Chilwa (lake) | E6 |
| Chinteche | D5 |
| Chiradzulu | E6 |
| Chiromo | E6 |
| Chitipa | C5 |
| Cholo | E6 |
| Dedza | D5 |
| Dowa | D5 |
| Karonga | C5 |
| Kasungu | D5 |
| Lilongwe | D5 |
| Livingstonia | D5 |
| Mangoche | D6 |
| Mulanje | E6 |
| Mzimba | D5 |
| Mzuzu | D5 |
| Ncheu | D5 |
| Nkhata Bay | D5 |
| Nkhota Kota | D5 |
| Nsanje | E6 |
| Nyasa (lake) | C5, D5 |
| Rumphi | D5 |
| Salima | D5 |
| Sapitwa (mount) | E6 |
| Shire (river) | E5, E6 |
| Zomba | E6 |

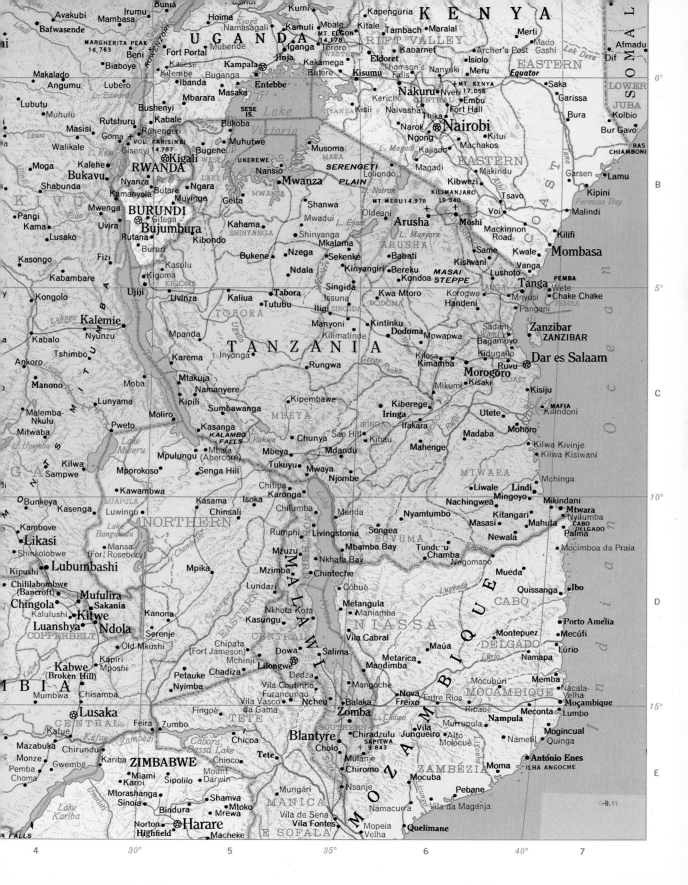

*The highveld*

# MINI-FACTS AT A GLANCE

## GENERAL INFORMATION

**Official Name:** Republic of Malawi

**Capital:** Lilongwe

**Official Language:** English and Chichewa: In cities and towns most people are fluent in English, but in rural areas, Chichewa is more common.

**Government:** Malawi is a one-party republic governed by the Malawi Congress party (MCP). Its constitution vests executive power in a president who is both head of state and head of the government. The Parliament consists of 75 members; 60 are elected and 15 are appointed by the president. Both elected officials and traditional chiefs are represented on district councils.

**National Song:** *"Mlungu dalitsani Maslawi"* ("God, Bless Our Land of Malawi")

**Flag:** The national flag is a horizontal tricolor of black, red, and green, with a red rising sun in the center of the black stripe.

**Money:** The kwacha (K) of 100 tambala (t) is the national currency. In 1989, K2.1022 equaled one U.S. dollar.

**Weights and Measures:** Malawi uses the metric system.

**Population:** 7,752,000 (1988 estimate); 12 percent urban, 88 percent rural

**Major Cities:**

| | |
|---|---|
| Blantyre | 355,200 |
| Lilongwe | 186,800 |
| Zomba | 53,000 |

(Population based on 1987 estimates)

**Religion:** About 65 percent of the people are nominally Christian and 16 percent are Muslims. The Roman Catholic, Anglican, Seventh-Day Adventist, and Presbyterian churches are long established and prominent. The majority practices traditional animistic religions along with other religions.

## GEOGRAPHY

**Highest Point:** The peak of Sapitwa in the Mulanje Mountains, 9,843 ft. (3,000 m)

**Lowest Point:** 121 ft. (37 m) on the southern border, where the Shire River approaches its confluence with the Zambezi River

**Mountains:** The highest areas are called the highveld. Among them are the Mulanje Mountains, Zomba Plateau, and Nyika Plateau.

**Lakes and Rivers:** Lake Malawi is the 3rd-largest lake in Africa and the 12th largest in the world. It is approximately 365 mi. (787 km) long and 52 mi. (84 km) at its widest point and covers 8,900 sq. mi. (23,051 km$^2$) The Shire, the major river, flows from the southern tip of Lake Malawi to join the Zambezi River in Mozambique.

**Climate:** Although Malawi has a distinctly temperate climate, variations in altitude lead to wide differences. In general the seasons may be divided into the hot, wet season, which lasts from October to April, and the rest of the year, which is relatively cold and dry.

**Greatest Distances:** North to south: 520 mi. (837 km)
East to west: 100 mi. (161 km)

**Area:** 45,747 sq. mi. (118,484 km$^2$)

## NATURE

**Trees:** About one-fourth of the land area is covered with forest or woodland, with indigenous softwoods in the better watered areas, bamboo and cedars on the Mulanje Mountains, and evergreen conifers in the highlands. Mopane, baobab, acacia, and mahogany trees are found at lower elevations. The most common type of vegetation is the indigenous brachystegia forest.

**Animals:** There are many varieties of animal life. The elephant, giraffe, black rhino, hippo, zebra, and buffalo are found in many areas. Hippopotamuses dwell on the shores of Lake Malawi. Many varieties of antelopes are found, as well as the baboon, monkey, hyena, wolf, zebra, lion, nocturnal cat, badger, and porcupine. Animals are protected in several game reserves and national parks, of which the Kasungu National Park is the largest.

Fish abound in the lakes and rivers. Lake Malawi has nearly 270 varieties. They include bass, catfish, perch, carp, and trout, as well as fish that are exported all over the world for aquariums.

**Birds:** There are at least 600 species of birds. The most striking is the majestic fish eagle, which resembles the American bald eagle. There are also a number of rare species, such as the striking bar-tailed trogon, the vanga flycatcher, and the sharpe's akalat.

## EVERYDAY LIFE

**Food:** Most Malawians depend on the products of a subsistence agriculture, mainly corn, cassava, and millet. The most common food is *nsima*, a kind of porridge, which is eaten with a spicy sauce called *ndiwo*. Sweet potatoes and pumpkins are popular also. Fish, usually sold dried, meat, and fowl are also basic foods.

**Housing:** The dwellings that make up traditional villages are small round or oblong thatch-covered buildings. They are made of dried mud, which keeps them cool even in the hot weather. In urban areas the European influence is strong. Houses on the edges of the cities are generally poor and crude and made of scrap materials.

### Holidays

January 1, New Year's Day
March 3, Martyr's Day
May 14, Kamuzu Day
July 6, Republic or National Day
First Monday in August, Bank Holiday
October 17, Mother's Day
December 21, National Tree Planting Day
December 25, Christmas Day
December 26, Boxing Day

**Culture:** Various traditional arts and crafts, notably sculpture in wood and ivory, are practiced widely. Oral folklore is produced for radio, while written folklore has remained less developed.

Written literature began in 1934 when Samuel Yosia Ntara published *Man in Africa*. Legson Kayira wrote an award-winning autobiography called *I Will Try*, three novels in English, and other stories in Chichewa.

Wood carving, basket and mat weaving, and pottery making have been developed both as art and as practical crafts.

The most common musical instrument is the drum. Malawian drumming is complex and intricate and is often accompanied by dancing.

**Transportation:** Landlocked Malawi is served by two railroads; one running from Limbe to Nacala and from Limbe southward to Beira, the other from Limbe to the lakeshore at Chipoka and Salima and then to Lilongwe. About a third of the roads are suitable for all kinds of weather.

The most important form of transportation in Malawi is water transport. Passenger and cargo boats ply the lake, and many use the canoes and dhows that carried their ancestors.

A government-owned airline, Air Malawi, provides both national and international service. Air transport is still very expensive and few Malawians can afford it. In fact most travel by foot, on bicycle, or on cheap buses.

**Communication:** All communication is strictly controlled by the government.

**Education:** Education is not required; the eight-year primary system has an enrollment of about 45 percent of school-age children. There are four-year secondary schools, technical and teacher-training institutes, and a university, the University of Malawi, which has an enrollment of more than 1,000 students. About 17 percent of the adult population is literate.

**Health and Welfare:** Malawi does not have a social security system, but other welfare programs provide assistance to children, the physically handicapped, and the indigent. Some medical services are provided free in government hospitals. The shortage of medical personnel is especially acute in rural areas. Malaria, tuberculosis, gastrointestinal diseases, and leprosy are the major health problems.

## ECONOMY AND INDUSTRY

**Principal Products:**
*Manufacturing:* Cement production; light consumer goods, including beer, blankets, cigarettes, soap, sugar; furniture construction; printing and publishing
*Agriculture:* Corn, peanuts, sunflower seeds, coffee, tea, cotton, tobacco
*Mining:* Gold

## IMPORTANT DATES

200 A.D.—The Bantu people are settled in Malawi

15th century—The Amaravi kingdom, centered in the Shire River valley, rises and continues to thrive

1600s—Mzura extends his power

18th century—The Amaravi kingdom declines due to warfare and internal conflicts

End of 18th century—Lake Malawi is one of the strongest centers of the slave trade in East Africa

1859—Dr. David Livingstone visits the area, paves the way for arrival of Scottish and British settlers and missionaries

1873—Livingstone dies

1880s and 1890s—Missionaries from the Dutch Reformed church of South Africa and the Roman Catholic church establish missions

1884—The African Lakes Corporation establishes a trading post at Karonga

1886—Mlozi moves into the land of the Ngonde and enslaves many and massacres those he cannot enslave

1888—War between Mlozi and African Lakes Corporation

1895—Mlozi is captured and executed; slave trade begins to decrease

1900s—The Reverend John Chilembwe returns to Nyasaland to start his mission, the Providence Industrial Mission

1907—British Protectorate of Nyasaland is created

1915—Chilembwe and his followers attack European settlers after some of Chilembwe's churches had been burned

1935—Nyasaland is linked to the coast by rail

1944—Nyasaland Congress party (NCP) formed

1953—Nyasaland becomes part of the Central African Federation, composed of Northern Rhodesia, Southern Rhodesia, and Nyasaland

1958—Dr. Hastings Banda returns to lead NCP

1963—The Federation is dissolved, Nyasaland is granted internal self-government, and Banda is named prime minister

1964—Independent nation of Malawi is declared

1966—Malawi becomes a republic with Dr. Hastings Kamuzu Banda its first president

1970s—President Banda adopts a policy that is tolerant of South Africa but often critical of the surrounding black African communities; Malawi becomes a haven for anti-government rebels from Mozambique

1978—First parliamentary elections since independence are held

Early 1980s—Banda remains in power as president; Malawi continues its close association with South Africa

*Dugout canoes in a swampy area on the grassy fringe of Lake Malawi*

## IMPORTANT PEOPLE

Dr. Hastings Kamuzu Banda (1898-    ), medical doctor, sole leader of Malawi since it was granted independence in 1964

The Reverend John Chilembwe (1870-1915), minister, founder of the Providence Industrial Mission

M. Masauko Chipembere (1930-75), one of the original leaders of the National Congress party

The Reverend Henry Henderson, established Church of Scotland mission at Blantyre in the Shire Highlands

Sir Harry Johnston (1858-1927), colonial commissioner for the British Central African Protectorate (Nyasaland); consolidated British government's position in Malawi; captured Mlozi; ended slave trade

Audrey Kachingwe (1926-    ), contemporary writer

Legson Kayira, contemporary writer of fiction and nonfiction

David Livingstone (1818-73), Scottish missionary and explorer in Africa; discovered Lake Nyasa (Malawi), 1859

Mlozi, infamous outlaw, half Arab, half Malawian, led gang of slave raiders in late-19th century; signed peace treaty with Sir Harry Hamilton Johnston

Mzura, powerful 17th-century chief, wise and strong leader

Samuel Yosia Ntara (1905-    ), writer, author of *Man in Africa* (1934)

David Rubadiri (1930-    ), contemporary writer

The Reverend D.C.R. Scott, missionary who built the Church of St. Michael and All Angels in 1892. Reached Malawi in 1881

Undi, chieftain who built up considerable power by 1700

Willy Zingani, contemporary writer

*A panoramic view from the Mulanje Mountains*

# INDEX

**Page numbers that appear in boldface type indicate illustrations**

## About the Author

Martha S.B. Lane grew up in Malawi where her parents worked as missionaries. She has a B.A. from Bowdoin College in Maine and a M.A. in African Studies from Northwestern University in Evanston, Illinois. Presently Ms. Lane is living in Zimbabwe, where she is on a Fulbright fellowship. She is working on her Ph.D. researching the role of literature and music in the African struggle for independence in Zimbabwe.